MznLnx

Missing Links Exam Preps

Exam Prep for

Prealgebra

Aufmann, Barker, Lockwwd, 4th Edition

The MznLnx Exam Prep is your link from the texbook and lecture to your exams.
The MznLnx Exam Preps are unauthorized and comprehensive reviews of your textbooks.

All material provided by MznLnx and Rico Publications (c) 2010
Textbook publishers and textbook authors do not particpate in or contribute to these reviews.

MznLnx

Rico
Publications

Exam Prep for Prealgebra
4th Edition
Aufmann, Barker, Lockwwd

Publisher: Raymond Houge
Assistant Editor: Michael Rouger
Text and Cover Designer: Lisa Buckner
Marketing Manager: Sara Swagger
Project Manager, Editorial Production: Jerry Emerson
Art Director: Vernon Lowerui

Product Manager: Dave Mason
Editorial Assitant: Rachel Guzmanji
Pedagogy: Debra Long
Cover Image: Jim Reed/Getty Images
Text and Cover Printer: City Printing, Inc.
Compositor: Media Mix, Inc.

(c) 2010 Rico Publications
ALL RIGHTS RESERVED. No part of this work covered by the copyright may be reproduced or used in any form or by an means--graphic, electronic, or mechanical, including photocopying, recording, taping, Web distribution, information storage, and retrieval systems, or in any other manner--without the written permission of the publisher.

For more information about our products, contact us at:

Dave.Mason@RicoPublications.com

For permission to use material from this text or

product, submit a request online to:

Dave.Mason@RicoPublications.com

Printed in the United States
ISBN:

Contents

CHAPTER 1
Whole Numbers 1
CHAPTER 2
Integers 19
CHAPTER 3
Fractions 28
CHAPTER 4
Decimals and Real Numbers 39
CHAPTER 5
Variable Expressions 49
CHAPTER 6
First-Degree Equations 60
CHAPTER 7
Measurement and Proportion 72
CHAPTER 8
Percent 79
CHAPTER 9
Geometry 85
CHAPTER 10
Statistics and Probability 109
ANSWER KEY 121

TO THE STUDENT

COMPREHENSIVE

The *MznLnx* Exam Prep series is designed to help you pass your exams. Editors at MznLnx review your textbooks and then prepare these practice exams to help you master the textbook material. Unlike study guides, workbooks, and practice tests provided by the texbook publisher and textbook authors, *MznLnx* gives you **all** of the material in each chapter in exam form, not just samples, so you can be sure to nail your exam.

MECHANICAL

The MznLnx Exam Prep series creates exams that will help you learn the subject matter as well as test you on your understanding. Each question is designed to help you master the concept. Just working through the exams, you gain an understanding of the subject--its a simple mechanical process that produces success.

INTEGRATED STUDY GUIDE AND REVIEW

MznLnx is not just a set of exams designed to test you, its also a comprehensive review of the subject content. Each exam question is also a review of the concept, making sure that you will get the answer correct without having to go to other sources of material. You learn as you go! Its the easiest way to pass an exam.

HUMOR

Studying can be tedious and dry. MznLnx's instructional design includes moderate humor within the exam questions on occassion, to break the tedium and revitalize the brain

Chapter 1. Whole Numbers

1. Exponentiation is a mathematical operation, written a^n, involving two numbers, the base a and the _____ n. When n is a positive integer, exponentiation corresponds to repeated multiplication:

$$a^n = \underbrace{a \times \cdots \times a}_{n},$$

just as multiplication by a positive integer corresponds to repeated addition:

$$a \times n = \underbrace{a + \cdots + a}_{n}.$$

The _____ is usually shown as a superscript to the right of the base. The exponentiation a^n can be read as: a raised to the n-th power, a raised to the power [of] n or possibly a raised to the _____ [of] n, or more briefly: a to the n-th power or a to the power [of] n, or even more briefly: a to the n.

   a. Exponent
   b. Exponentiating by squaring
   c. Exponential sum
   d. Exponential tree

2. A _____ is one of the basic shapes of geometry: a polygon with three corners or vertices and three sides or edges which are line segments. A _____ with vertices A, B, and C is denoted ABC.

In Euclidean geometry any three non-collinear points determine a unique _____ and a unique plane.

   a. Kepler triangle
   b. Triangle
   c. 1-center problem
   d. Fuhrmann circle

3. In mathematics, a _____ can mean either an element of the set {1, 2, 3, ...} or an element of the set {0, 1, 2, 3, ...}. The latter is especially preferred in mathematical logic, set theory, and computer science.

_____s have two main purposes: they can be used for counting, and they can be used for ordering.

   a. Strong partition cardinal
   b. Suslin cardinal
   c. Cardinal numbers
   d. Natural number

4. In mathematics, an inequality is a statement about the relative size or order of two objects. For example 14 > 10, or 14 is _____ 10. The notation a > b means that a is _____ b and 'a' would be to the right of 'b' on a number line.
   a. Cauchy-Schwarz inequality
   b. FKG inequality
   c. Greater than
   d. Minkowski inequality

5. In mathematics, an _____ is a statement about the relative size or order of two objects, or about whether they are the same or not

   - The notation a < b means that a is less than b.
   - The notation a > b means that a is greater than b.
   - The notation a ≠ b means that a is not equal to b, but does not say that one is bigger than the other or even that they can be compared in size.

In all these cases, a is not equal to b, hence, '_____'.

These relations are known as strict _____

   - The notation a ≤ b means that a is less than or equal to b;
   - The notation a ≥ b means that a is greater than or equal to b;

An additional use of the notation is to show that one quantity is much greater than another, normally by several orders of magnitude.

   - The notation a << b means that a is much less than b.
   - The notation a >> b means that a is much greater than b.

If the sense of the _____ is the same for all values of the variables for which its members are defined, then the _____ is called an 'absolute' or 'unconditional' _____. If the sense of an _____ holds only for certain values of the variables involved, but is reversed or destroyed for other values of the variables, it is called a conditional _____.

An _____ may appear unsolvable because it only states whether a number is larger or smaller than another number; but it is possible to apply the same operations for equalities to inequalities. For example, to find x for the _____ 10x > 23 one would divide 23 by 10.

   a. A Mathematical Theory of Communication
   b. A chemical equation
   c. Inequality
   d. A posteriori

Chapter 1. Whole Numbers

6. _____ is the mathematical operation of scaling one number by another. It is one of the four basic operations in elementary arithmetic.

_____ is defined for whole numbers in terms of repeated addition; for example, 4 multiplied by 3 can be calculated by adding 3 copies of 4 together:

$$4 + 4 + 4 = 12.$$

_____ of rational numbers and real numbers is defined by systematic generalization of this basic idea.

   a. The number 0 is even.
   b. Least common multiple
   c. Multiplication
   d. Highest common factor

7. In mathematics, a _____ is a picture of a straight line in which the integers are shown as specially-marked points evenly spaced on the line. Although this image only shows the integers from -9 to 9, the line includes all real numbers, continuing 'forever' in each direction. It is often used as an aid in teaching simple addition and subtraction, especially involving negative numbers.
   a. Number line
   b. Real number
   c. Number system
   d. Point plotting

8. In mathematics, an _____ in the sense of ring theory is a subring $\mathcal{O}$ of a ring R that satisfies the conditions

   1. R is a ring which is a finite-dimensional algebra over the rational number field $\mathbb{Q}$
   2. $\mathcal{O}$ spans R over $\mathbb{Q}$, so that $\mathbb{Q}\mathcal{O} = R$, and
   3. $\mathcal{O}$ is a lattice in R.

The third condition can be stated more accurately, in terms of the extension of scalars of R to the real numbers, embedding R in a real vector space. In less formal terms, additively $\mathcal{O}$ should be a free abelian group generated by a basis for R over $\mathbb{Q}$.

The leading example is the case where R is a number field K and $\mathcal{O}$ is its ring of integers. In algebraic number theory there are examples for any K other than the rational field of proper subrings of the ring of integers that are also _____ s.

a. Annihilator
b. Algebraic
c. Efficiency
d. Order

9. In algebra and computer programming, when a number or expression is both preceded and followed by a binary operation, a rule is required for which operation should be applied first; this rule is known as an _____ . From the earliest use of mathematical notation, multiplication took precedence over addition, whichever side of a number it appeared on. Thus 3 + 4 × 5 = 5 × 4 + 3 = 23.

a. Order of Operations
b. Isomorphism class
c. Algebraic K-theory
d. Identity element

10. In mathematics, a _____ can mean either an element of the set {1, 2, 3, ...} (i.e the positive integers) or an element of the set {0, 1, 2, 3, ...} (i.e. the non-negative integers).

a. Bounded
b. Degrees of freedom
c. Whole number
d. FISH

11. In mathematics, the _____ of a real number is its numerical value without regard to its sign. So, for example, 3 is the _____ of both 3 and −3.

The _____ of a number a is denoted by | a | .

Generalizations of the _____ for real numbers occur in a wide variety of mathematical settings.

a. A Mathematical Theory of Communication
b. Area hyperbolic functions
c. A chemical equation
d. Absolute value

12. A _____ is a software program that facilitates symbolic mathematics. The core functionality of a CAS is manipulation of mathematical expressions in symbolic form.

The symbolic manipulations supported typically include

- simplification to the smallest possible expression or some standard form, including automatic simplification with assumptions and simplification with constraints
- substitution of symbolic, functors or numeric values for expressions
- change of form of expressions: expanding products and powers, partial and full factorization, rewriting as partial fractions, constraint satisfaction, rewriting trigonometric functions as exponentials, etc.
- partial and total differentiation
- symbolic constrained and unconstrained global optimization
- solution of linear and some non-linear equations over various domains
- solution of some differential and difference equations
- taking some limits
- some indefinite and definite integration, including multidimensional integrals
- integral transforms
- arbitrary-precision numeric operations
- Series operations such as expansion, summation and products
- matrix operations including products, inverses, etc.
- display of mathematical expressions in two-dimensional mathematical form, often using typesetting systems similar to TeX
- add-ons for use in applied mathematics such as physics packages for physical computation
- plotting graphs and parametric plots of functions in two and three dimensions, and animating them
- APIs for linking it on an external program such as a database, or using in a programming language to use the _____
- drawing charts and diagrams
- string manipulation such as matching and searching
- statistical computation
- Theorem proving and verification
- graphic production and editing such as CGI and signal processing as image processing
- sound synthesis

Many also include a programming language, allowing users to implement their own algorithms.

Some _____s focus on a specific area of application; these are typically developed in academia and are free.

a. Computer algebra system
b. 120-cell
c. 1-center problem
d. 2-3 heap

13. A bar chart or _____ is a chart with rectangular bars with lengths proportional to the values that they represent. Bar charts are used for comparing two or more values. The bars can be horizontally or vertically oriented.

a. 1-center problem
b. 2-3 heap
c. 120-cell
d. Bar graph

14. In mathematics, a _____ is a number that can be expressed as an integral of an algebraic function over an algebraic domain. Kontsevich and Zagier define a _____ as a complex number whose real and imaginary parts are values of absolutely convergent integrals of rational functions with rational coefficients, over domains in given by polynomial inequalities with rational coefficients.
    a. Closeness
    b. Period
    c. Boussinesq approximation
    d. Disk

15. _____ is a numeral system in which each position is related to the next by a constant multiplier, a common ratio, called the base or radix of that numeral system.
    a. NegaFibonacci coding
    b. Place value
    c. Negative base
    d. Cyrillic numerals

16. _____ involves reducing the number of significant digits in a number. The result of _____ is a 'shorter' number having fewer non-zero digits yet similar in magnitude. The result is less precise but easier to use.
    a. Shabakh
    b. Sudan function
    c. Hyper operator
    d. Rounding

17. _____, also sometimes known as standard form or as exponential notation, is a way of writing numbers that accommodates values too large or small to be conveniently written in standard decimal notation. _____ has a number of useful properties and is often favored by scientists, mathematicians and engineers, who work with such numbers.

In _____, numbers are written in the form:

$$a \times 10^b$$

a. 1-center problem
b. Leading zero
c. Radix point
d. Scientific notation

18. _____ is simply the manner of writing out an expression in full. When a quantity is written as a sum of terms, or as a continued product, _____ notation is used to illustrate the expression in its entirety.

a. Algebraic element
b. Algebraic function
c. Expanded form
d. Algebra

19. A _____ is a simple shape of Euclidean geometry consisting of those points in a plane which are at a constant distance, called the radius, from a fixed point, called the center. A _____ with center A is sometimes denoted by the symbol A.

A chord of a _____ is a line segment whose two endpoints lie on the _____.

a. Circumcircle
b. Malfatti circles
c. Circular segment
d. Circle

20. In graph theory, a _____ is a graph whose vertices can be associated with chords of a circle such that two vertices are adjacent if and only if the corresponding chords in the circle intersect.

Spinrad (1994) gives an $O(n^2)$-time recognition algorithm for _____s that also computes a circle model of the input graph if it is a _____.

A number of other problems that are NP-complete on general graphs have polynomial time algorithms when restricted to _____s.

a. Planar graph
b. Vertex-transitive graph
c. Sparse graph
d. Circle graph

21. _____ or pictograph is a symbol representing a concept, object, activity, place or event by illustration. Pictography is a form of writing in which ideas are transmitted through drawing. It is a basis of cuneiform and, to some extent, hieroglyphic writing, which uses drawings also as phonetic letters or determinative rhymes.
   a. Treemapping
   b. Pictographs
   c. Sparkline
   d. Pictogram

22. A _____ is the result of applying a function to a set of data.

More formally, statistical theory defines a _____ as a function of a sample where the function itself is independent of the sample's distribution: the term is used both for the function and for the value of the function on a given sample.

A _____ is distinct from an unknown statistical parameter, which is not computable from a sample.

   a. Statistic
   b. Loss function
   c. Spatial dependence
   d. Parameter space

23. _____ is a mathematical science pertaining to the collection, analysis, interpretation or explanation, and presentation of data. It also provides tools for prediction and forecasting based on data. It is applicable to a wide variety of academic disciplines, from the natural and social sciences to the humanities, government and business.
   a. Probability distribution
   b. Regression toward the mean
   c. Percentile rank
   d. Statistics

24. _____: A graph using line segments to join the plotted points to represent data over time.
   a. Closed under some operation
   b. Conditional factor demand
   c. Broken-line graph
   d. Control theory

25. An _____ is a number which is involved in addition. A number being added is considered to be an _____.

a. A posteriori
b. A chemical equation
c. Addend
d. A Mathematical Theory of Communication

26. In mathematics, _____ is a property that a binary operation can have. It means that, within an expression containing two or more of the same associative operators in a row, the order that the operations are performed does not matter as long as the sequence of the operands is not changed. That is, rearranging the parentheses in such an expression will not change its value.
   a. Idempotence
   b. Unital
   c. Algebraically closed
   d. Associativity

27. A _____ is a device for performing mathematical calculations, distinguished from a computer by having a limited problem solving ability and an interface optimized for interactive calculation rather than programming. _____s can be hardware or software, and mechanical or electronic, and are often built into devices such as PDAs or mobile phones.

Modern electronic _____s are generally small, digital, and usually inexpensive.

   a. 1-center problem
   b. 2-3 heap
   c. 120-cell
   d. Calculator

28. Any mathematical statement that contains a variable is a _____.
   a. Convex and concave
   b. Classification of the finite simple groups
   c. Complex Mexican hat wavelet
   d. Variable expression

29. _____ is the calculated approximation of a result which is usable even if input data may be incomplete or uncertain.

In statistics, see _____ theory, estimator.

In mathematics, approximation or _____ typically means finding upper or lower bounds of a quantity that cannot readily be computed precisely and is also an educated guess .

a. Estimator
b. U-statistic
c. Estimation
d. Estimation theory

30. The _____ is a rule which states that when you add or multiply numbers, changing the order doesn't change the result.
a. Conditional event algebra
b. Semigroupoid
c. Coimage
d. Commutative law

31. The traditional names for the parts of the formula c − b = a, are _____ (c) − subtrahend (b) = difference (a). The words _____ and subtrahend are uncommon in modern usage. Instead we say that c and −b are terms, and treat subtraction as addition of the opposite. The answer is still called the difference.
a. Multiplication
b. Lowest common denominator
c. Plus and minus signs
d. Minuend

32. The quantity that is deducted from the minuend in subtraction is the _____.
a. Trailing zeros
b. Lowest common denominator
c. The number 0 is even.
d. Subtrahend

33. In geometry and trigonometry, an _____ is the figure formed by two rays sharing a common endpoint, called the vertex of the _____. The magnitude of the _____ is the 'amount of rotation' that separates the two rays, and can be measured by considering the length of circular arc swept out when one ray is rotated about the vertex to coincide with the other. Where there is no possibility of confusion, the term '_____' is used interchangeably for both the geometric configuration itself and for its angular magnitude.
a. A Mathematical Theory of Communication
b. A posteriori
c. Angle
d. A chemical equation

Chapter 1. Whole Numbers

34. _____ is a part of mathematics concerned with questions of size, shape, and relative position of figures and with properties of space. _____ is one of the oldest sciences. Initially a body of practical knowledge concerning lengths, areas, and volumes, in the third century BC _____ was put into an axiomatic form by Euclid, whose treatment--Euclidean _____--set a standard for many centuries to follow.
   a. 120-cell
   b. Geometry
   c. 2-3 heap
   d. 1-center problem

35. In geometry, a _____ is a part of a line that is bounded by two distinct end points, and contains every point on the line between its end points. Examples of _____s include the sides of a triangle or square. More generally, when the end points are both vertices of a polygon, the _____ is either an edge if they are adjacent vertices, or otherwise a diagonal.
   a. Cuboid
   b. Golden angle
   c. Transversal line
   d. Line segment

36. In mathematics the concept of a _____ generalizes notions such as 'length', 'area', and 'volume'. Informally, given some base set, a '_____' is any consistent assignment of 'sizes' to the subsets of the base set. Depending on the application, the 'size' of a subset may be interpreted as its physical size, the amount of something that lies within the subset, or the probability that some random process will yield a result within the subset.
   a. Cusp
   b. Lattice
   c. Congruent
   d. Measure

37. A _____ of a curve is the envelope of a family of congruent circles centered on the curve. It generalises the concept of _____ lines.

It is sometimes called the offset curve but the term 'offset' often refers also to translation.

   a. Parallel
   b. Cycloid
   c. Bifolium
   d. Cissoid

38. The existence and properties of _____ are the basis of Euclid's parallel postulate. _____ are two lines on the same plane that do not intersect even assuming that lines extend to infinity in either direction.

a. Parallel lines
b. Spidron
c. Vertical translation
d. Square wheel

39. In mathematics, a _____ is, informally, an infinitely vast and infinitely thin sheet. _____s may be thought of as objects in some higher dimensional space, or they may be considered without any outside space, as in the setting of Euclidean geometry
a. Plane
b. Blocking
c. Bandwidth
d. Group

40. In geometry a _____ is traditionally a plane figure that is bounded by a closed path or circuit, composed of a finite sequence of straight line segments. These segments are called its edges or sides, and the points where two edges meet are the _____'s vertices or corners. The interior of the _____ is sometimes called its body.
a. Regular polygon
b. Parallelogon
c. Polygonal curve
d. Polygon

41. In geometry and trigonometry, a _____ is defined as an angle between two straight intersecting lines of ninety degrees, or one-quarter of a circle.
a. Sine integral
b. Right angle
c. Trigonometry
d. Trigonometric functions

42. In mathematics, the _____ is an approach to finding a particular solution to certain inhomogeneous ordinary differential equations and recurrence relations. It is closely related to the annihilator method, but instead of using a particular kind of differential operator in order to find the best possible form of the particular solution, a 'guess' is made as to the appropriate form, which is then tested by differentiating the resulting equation. In this sense, the _____ is less formal but more intuitive than the annihilator method.

a. Differential algebraic equations
b. Linear differential equation
c. Method of undetermined coefficients
d. Phase line

43. The _____ is the length of the line that bounds an area In the special case where the area is circular, the _____ is known as the circumference.
   a. Reflection symmetry
   b. Multilateration
   c. Concyclic
   d. Perimeter

44. In geometry, a _____ is a polygon with four sides or edges and four vertices or corners. Sometimes, the term quadrangle is used, for etymological symmetry with triangle, and sometimes tetragon for consistency with pentagon, hexagon and so on. The interior angles of a _____ add up to 360 degrees of arc.
   a. 120-cell
   b. Quadrilateral
   c. 2-3 heap
   d. 1-center problem

45. In geometry, a _____ is defined as a quadrilateral where all four of its angles are right angles.
   a. Polytope
   b. Rectangle
   c. Cantor-Dedekind axiom
   d. Point group in two dimensions

46. In computational complexity theory, an algorithm is said to take _____ if the asymptotic upper bound for the time it requires is proportional to the size of the input, which is usually denoted n.

Informally spoken, the running time increases linearly with the size of the input. For example, a procedure that adds up all elements of a list requires time proportional to the length of the list.

   a. Time-constructible function
   b. Truth table reduction
   c. Constructible function
   d. Linear time

47. In mathematics, the _____ of a number n is the number that, when added to n, yields zero. The _____ of n is denoted −n. For example, 7 is −7, because 7 + (−7) = 0, and the _____ of −0.3 is 0.3, because −0.3 + 0.3 = 0.
   a. Associativity
   b. Additive inverse
   c. Arity
   d. Algebraic structure

48. In mathematics and computer science, _____ (also base-16, hexa or base, of 16. It uses sixteen distinct symbols, most often the symbols 0-9 to represent values zero to nine, and A, B, C, D, E, F (or a through f) to represent values ten to fifteen.

Its primary use is as a human friendly representation of binary coded values, so it is often used in digital electronics and computer engineering.

   a. Hexadecimal
   b. Factoradic
   c. Radix
   d. Tetradecimal

49. A _____ is a three-dimensional geometric shape that tapers smoothly from a flat, round base to a point called the apex or vertex. More precisely, it is the solid figure bounded by a plane base and the surface formed by the locus of all straight line segments joining the apex to the perimeter of the base. The term '_____' sometimes refers just to the surface of this solid figure, or just to the lateral surface.
   a. Characteristic
   b. Cone
   c. Gravity waves
   d. Blocking

50. A _____ is the large number 10^{100}, that is, the digit 1 followed by one hundred zeros. The term was coined in 1938 by Milton Sirotta, nephew of American mathematician Edward Kasner. Kasner popularized the concept in his book Mathematics and the Imagination.
   a. 1-center problem
   b. 120-cell
   c. 2-3 heap
   d. Googol

51. _____s are payments made by a corporation to its shareholder members. When a corporation earns a profit or surplus, that money can be put to two uses: it can either be re-invested in the business, or it can be paid to the shareholders as a _____. Many corporations retain a portion of their earnings and pay the remainder as a _____.
   a. 1-center problem
   b. Dividend
   c. GNU Privacy Guard
   d. 120-cell

52. In mathematics, a _____ of an integer n is an integer which evenly divides n without leaving a remainder.

For example, 7 is a _____ of 42 because 42/7 = 6. We also say 42 is divisible by 7 or 42 is a multiple of 7 or 7 divides 42 or 7 is a factor of 42 and we usually write 7 | 42.

   a. 2-3 heap
   b. 120-cell
   c. 1-center problem
   d. Divisor

53. In mathematics, a _____ is the end result of a division problem. It can also be expressed as the number of times the divisor divides into the dividend.
   a. Notation
   b. Quotient
   c. Marginal cost
   d. Limiting

54. In mathematics, a division is called a _____ if the divisor is zero. Such a division can be formally expressed as $\frac{a}{0}$ where a is the dividend. Whether this expression can be assigned a well-defined value depends upon the mathematical setting.
   a. 1-center problem
   b. Division by zero
   c. 120-cell
   d. 2-3 heap

55. In mathematics, an _____ or excessive number is a number n for which σσσ− 2n is called the abundance of n.

a. Abundant number
b. Integer sequence
c. Idoneal number
d. Unitary perfect number

56. A _____ number is a positive integer which has a positive divisor other than one or itself. By definition, every integer greater than one is either a prime number or a _____ number.zero and one are considered to be neither prime nor _____. For example, the integer 14 is a _____ number because it can be factored as 2 × 7.
a. Composite
b. Key server
c. Basis
d. Discontinuity

57. A _____ is a positive integer which has a positive divisor other than one or itself. In other words, if 0 < n is an integer and there are integers 1 < a, b < n such that n = a × b then n is composite. By definition, every integer greater than one is either a prime number or a _____.
a. Prime Pages
b. Ruth-Aaron pair
c. Megaprime
d. Composite number

58. In mathematics, in the realm of group theory, a group is said to be _____ if it equals its own commutator subgroup if the group has no nontrivial abelian quotients.

The smallest _____ group is the alternating group A_5. More generally, any non-abelian simple group is _____ since the commutator subgroup is a normal subgroup with abelian quotient.

a. Quaternion group
b. Free product
c. Group of Lie type
d. Perfect

59. In mathematics, a _____ is defined as a positive integer which is the sum of its proper positive divisors, that is, the sum of the positive divisors excluding the number itself. Equivalently, a _____ is a number that is half the sum of all of its positive divisors, or = 2n.

The first _____ is 6, because 1, 2, and 3 are its proper positive divisors, and 1 + 2 + 3 = 6.

Chapter 1. Whole Numbers   17

   a. Nonhypotenuse number
   b. Leonardo numbers
   c. Blum integer
   d. Perfect number

60. In mathematics, a _____ is a natural number which has exactly two distinct natural number divisors: 1 and itself. An infinitude of _____s exists, as demonstrated by Euclid around 300 BC. The first twenty-five _____s are:

   2, 3, 5, 7, 11, 13, 17, 19, 23, 29, 31, 37, 41, 43, 47, 53, 59, 61, 67, 71, 73, 79, 83, 89, 97.

   a. Pronic number
   b. Perrin number
   c. Highly composite number
   d. Prime number

61. In number theory, the _____s of a positive integer are the prime numbers that divide into that integer exactly, without leaving a remainder. The process of finding these numbers is called integer factorization, or prime factorization.

For a _____ p of n, the multiplicity of p is the largest exponent a for which p^a divides n.

   a. Cunningham chain
   b. Wieferich pair
   c. Gigantic prime
   d. Prime Factor

62. _____ is a quantity expressing the two-dimensional size of a defined part of a surface, typically a region bounded by a closed curve. The term surface _____ refers to the total _____ of the exposed surface of a 3-dimensional solid, such as the sum of the _____s of the exposed sides of a polyhedron. _____ is an important invariant in the differential geometry of surfaces.
   a. A chemical equation
   b. A Mathematical Theory of Communication
   c. A posteriori
   d. Area

63. In mathematics, and in particular in abstract algebra, distributivity is a property of binary operations that generalises the _____ law from elementary algebra.

a. General linear group
b. Closure with a twist
c. Distributive
d. Permutation

64. In mathematics, a _____ is an algebraic structure consisting of a set together with an operation that combines any two of its elements to form a third element. To qualify as a _____, the set and operation must satisfy a few conditions called _____ axioms, namely associativity, identity and invertibility. While these are familiar from many mathematical structures, such as number systems--for example, the integers endowed with the addition operation form a _____--the formulation of the axioms is detached from the concrete nature of the _____ and its operation.
  a. Characteristic function
  b. Coherence
  c. Derivative algebra
  d. Group

65. A _____, from the French patron, is a type of theme of recurring events of or objects, sometimes referred to as elements of a set. These elements repeat in a predictable manner. It can be a template or model which can be used to generate things or parts of a thing, especially if the things that are created have enough in common for the underlying _____ to be inferred, in which case the things are said to exhibit the unique _____.
  a. 2-3 heap
  b. 120-cell
  c. 1-center problem
  d. Pattern

Chapter 2. Integers

1. Exponentiation is a mathematical operation, written a^n, involving two numbers, the base a and the _____ n. When n is a positive integer, exponentiation corresponds to repeated multiplication:

$$a^n = \underbrace{a \times \cdots \times a}_{n},$$

just as multiplication by a positive integer corresponds to repeated addition:

$$a \times n = \underbrace{a + \cdots + a}_{n}.$$

The _____ is usually shown as a superscript to the right of the base. The exponentiation a^n can be read as: a raised to the n-th power, a raised to the power [of] n or possibly a raised to the _____ [of] n, or more briefly: a to the n-th power or a to the power [of] n, or even more briefly: a to the n.

   a. Exponential tree
   b. Exponential sum
   c. Exponentiating by squaring
   d. Exponent

2. A _____ is one of the basic shapes of geometry: a polygon with three corners or vertices and three sides or edges which are line segments. A _____ with vertices A, B, and C is denoted ABC.

In Euclidean geometry any three non-collinear points determine a unique _____ and a unique plane.

   a. Fuhrmann circle
   b. 1-center problem
   c. Kepler triangle
   d. Triangle

3. In mathematics, an inequality is a statement about the relative size or order of two objects. For example 14 > 10, or 14 is _____ 10. The notation a > b means that a is _____ b and 'a' would be to the right of 'b' on a number line.
   a. Minkowski inequality
   b. FKG inequality
   c. Cauchy-Schwarz inequality
   d. Greater than

4. In mathematics, an _____ is a statement about the relative size or order of two objects, or about whether they are the same or not

- The notation a < b means that a is less than b.
- The notation a > b means that a is greater than b.
- The notation a ≠ b means that a is not equal to b, but does not say that one is bigger than the other or even that they can be compared in size.

In all these cases, a is not equal to b, hence, '_____'.

These relations are known as strict _____

- The notation a ≤ b means that a is less than or equal to b;
- The notation a ≥ b means that a is greater than or equal to b;

An additional use of the notation is to show that one quantity is much greater than another, normally by several orders of magnitude.

- The notation a << b means that a is much less than b.
- The notation a >> b means that a is much greater than b.

If the sense of the _____ is the same for all values of the variables for which its members are defined, then the _____ is called an 'absolute' or 'unconditional' _____. If the sense of an _____ holds only for certain values of the variables involved, but is reversed or destroyed for other values of the variables, it is called a conditional _____.

An _____ may appear unsolvable because it only states whether a number is larger or smaller than another number; but it is possible to apply the same operations for equalities to inequalities. For example, to find x for the _____ 10x > 23 one would divide 23 by 10.

a. A chemical equation
b. A Mathematical Theory of Communication
c. Inequality
d. A posteriori

5. The _____ are the set of numbers consisting of the natural numbers including 0 and their negatives. They are numbers that can be written without a fractional or decimal component, and fall within the set {... −2, −1, 0, 1, 2, ...}.
a. Integers
b. A chemical equation
c. A Mathematical Theory of Communication
d. A posteriori

Chapter 2. Integers

6. In mathematics, a _____ is a picture of a straight line in which the integers are shown as specially-marked points evenly spaced on the line. Although this image only shows the integers from -9 to 9, the line includes all real numbers, continuing 'forever' in each direction. It is often used as an aid in teaching simple addition and subtraction, especially involving negative numbers.
    a. Point plotting
    b. Real number
    c. Number system
    d. Number line

7. In mathematics, an _____ in the sense of ring theory is a subring $\mathcal{O}$ of a ring R that satisfies the conditions

    1. R is a ring which is a finite-dimensional algebra over the rational number field $\mathbb{Q}$
    2. $\mathcal{O}$ spans R over $\mathbb{Q}$, so that $\mathbb{Q}\mathcal{O} = R$, and
    3. $\mathcal{O}$ is a lattice in R.

    The third condition can be stated more accurately, in terms of the extension of scalars of R to the real numbers, embedding R in a real vector space. In less formal terms, additively $\mathcal{O}$ should be a free abelian group generated by a basis for R over $\mathbb{Q}$.

    The leading example is the case where R is a number field K and $\mathcal{O}$ is its ring of integers. In algebraic number theory there are examples for any K other than the rational field of proper subrings of the ring of integers that are also _____ s.

    a. Order
    b. Annihilator
    c. Efficiency
    d. Algebraic

8. In algebra and computer programming, when a number or expression is both preceded and followed by a binary operation, a rule is required for which operation should be applied first; this rule is known as an _____ . From the earliest use of mathematical notation, multiplication took precedence over addition, whichever side of a number it appeared on. Thus 3 + 4 × 5 = 5 × 4 + 3 = 23.
    a. Algebraic K-theory
    b. Isomorphism class
    c. Identity element
    d. Order of Operations

9. In mathematics, the _____ of a Euclidean space is a special point, usually denoted by the letter O, used as a fixed point of reference for the geometry of the surrounding space. In a Cartesian coordinate system, the _____ is the point where the axes of the system intersect. In Euclidean geometry, the _____ may be chosen freely as any convenient point of reference.
   a. OMAC
   b. Autonomous system
   c. Interval
   d. Origin

10. In mathematics, the _____ of a real number is its numerical value without regard to its sign. So, for example, 3 is the _____ of both 3 and −3.

The _____ of a number a is denoted by $|a|$.

Generalizations of the _____ for real numbers occur in a wide variety of mathematical settings.

   a. A Mathematical Theory of Communication
   b. Area hyperbolic functions
   c. A chemical equation
   d. Absolute value

11. A _____ is a software program that facilitates symbolic mathematics. The core functionality of a CAS is manipulation of mathematical expressions in symbolic form.

The symbolic manipulations supported typically include

- simplification to the smallest possible expression or some standard form, including automatic simplification with assumptions and simplification with constraints
- substitution of symbolic, functors or numeric values for expressions
- change of form of expressions: expanding products and powers, partial and full factorization, rewriting as partial fractions, constraint satisfaction, rewriting trigonometric functions as exponentials, etc.
- partial and total differentiation
- symbolic constrained and unconstrained global optimization
- solution of linear and some non-linear equations over various domains
- solution of some differential and difference equations
- taking some limits
- some indefinite and definite integration, including multidimensional integrals
- integral transforms
- arbitrary-precision numeric operations
- Series operations such as expansion, summation and products
- matrix operations including products, inverses, etc.
- display of mathematical expressions in two-dimensional mathematical form, often using typesetting systems similar to TeX
- add-ons for use in applied mathematics such as physics packages for physical computation
- plotting graphs and parametric plots of functions in two and three dimensions, and animating them
- APIs for linking it on an external program such as a database, or using in a programming language to use the _____
- drawing charts and diagrams
- string manipulation such as matching and searching
- statistical computation
- Theorem proving and verification
- graphic production and editing such as CGI and signal processing as image processing
- sound synthesis

Many also include a programming language, allowing users to implement their own algorithms.

Some _____s focus on a specific area of application; these are typically developed in academia and are free.

a. 120-cell
b. 1-center problem
c. 2-3 heap
d. Computer algebra system

12. A bar chart or _____ is a chart with rectangular bars with lengths proportional to the values that they represent. Bar charts are used for comparing two or more values. The bars can be horizontally or vertically oriented.

a. Bar graph
b. 1-center problem
c. 2-3 heap
d. 120-cell

13. A _____ is a device for performing mathematical calculations, distinguished from a computer by having a limited problem solving ability and an interface optimized for interactive calculation rather than programming. _____s can be hardware or software, and mechanical or electronic, and are often built into devices such as PDAs or mobile phones.

Modern electronic _____s are generally small, digital, and usually inexpensive.

a. 120-cell
b. 2-3 heap
c. 1-center problem
d. Calculator

14. In mathematics, the _____ of a number n is the number that, when added to n, yields zero. The _____ of n is denoted −n. For example, 7 is −7, because 7 + (−7) = 0, and the _____ of −0.3 is 0.3, because −0.3 + 0.3 = 0.
a. Associativity
b. Additive inverse
c. Arity
d. Algebraic structure

15. The _____ is a rule which states that when you add or multiply numbers, changing the order doesn't change the result.
a. Conditional event algebra
b. Coimage
c. Semigroupoid
d. Commutative law

16. In mathematics, _____ is a property that a binary operation can have. It means that, within an expression containing two or more of the same associative operators in a row, the order that the operations are performed does not matter as long as the sequence of the operands is not changed. That is, rearranging the parentheses in such an expression will not change its value.

a. Associativity
b. Idempotence
c. Algebraically closed
d. Unital

17. Any mathematical statement that contains a variable is a _____.
a. Variable expression
b. Classification of the finite simple groups
c. Convex and concave
d. Complex Mexican hat wavelet

18. In mathematics, and in particular in abstract algebra, distributivity is a property of binary operations that generalises the _____ law from elementary algebra.
a. Closure with a twist
b. Permutation
c. General linear group
d. Distributive

19. _____ is the mathematical operation of scaling one number by another. It is one of the four basic operations in elementary arithmetic.

_____ is defined for whole numbers in terms of repeated addition; for example, 4 multiplied by 3 can be calculated by adding 3 copies of 4 together:

$$4 + 4 + 4 = 12.$$

_____ of rational numbers and real numbers is defined by systematic generalization of this basic idea.

a. Least common multiple
b. The number 0 is even.
c. Highest common factor
d. Multiplication

20. In mathematics, a _____ is an algebraic structure consisting of a set together with an operation that combines any two of its elements to form a third element. To qualify as a _____, the set and operation must satisfy a few conditions called _____ axioms, namely associativity, identity and invertibility. While these are familiar from many mathematical structures, such as number systems--for example, the integers endowed with the addition operation form a _____--the formulation of the axioms is detached from the concrete nature of the _____ and its operation.

Chapter 2. Integers

a. Characteristic function
b. Coherence
c. Derivative algebra
d. Group

21. In computational complexity theory, an algorithm is said to take _____ if the asymptotic upper bound for the time it requires is proportional to the size of the input, which is usually denoted n.

Informally spoken, the running time increases linearly with the size of the input. For example, a procedure that adds up all elements of a list requires time proportional to the length of the list.

a. Truth table reduction
b. Time-constructible function
c. Constructible function
d. Linear time

22. In mathematics, a set is said to be _____ if the operation on members of the set produces a member of the set. For example, the real numbers are closed under subtraction, but the natural numbers are not: 3 and 7 are both natural numbers, but the result of 3 − 7 is not.

Similarly, a set is said to be closed under a collection of operations if it is closed under each of the operations individually.

a. Contingency table
b. Continuous linear extension
c. Control chart
d. Closed under some operation

23. In mathematics and computer science, _____ (also base-16, hexa or base, of 16. It uses sixteen distinct symbols, most often the symbols 0-9 to represent values zero to nine, and A, B, C, D, E, F (or a through f) to represent values ten to fifteen.

Its primary use is as a human friendly representation of binary coded values, so it is often used in digital electronics and computer engineering.

a. Radix
b. Factoradic
c. Tetradecimal
d. Hexadecimal

24. In information theory, a _____ is a function mapping an alphabet to non-negative real numbers, satisfying a generalization of Kraft's inequality. A _____ page, a type of character encoding table, is one such _____.
a. Link encryption
b. File Camouflage
c. Code
d. Deterministic encryption

25. The _____ is a positional numeral system; it has positions for units, tens, hundreds, etc. The position of each digit conveys the multiplier (a power of ten) to be used with that digit—each position has a value ten times that of the position to its right.
a. Free
b. Composite
c. Cleaver
d. Decimal system

26. In mathematics, a _____ is a set of numbers,, together with one or more operations, such as addition or multiplication.

Examples of _____s include: natural numbers, integers, rational numbers, algebraic numbers, real numbers, complex numbers, p-adic numbers, surreal numbers, and hyperreal numbers.

a. Number line
b. Tally marks
c. Slope
d. Number system

1. Exponentiation is a mathematical operation, written a^n, involving two numbers, the base a and the _____ n. When n is a positive integer, exponentiation corresponds to repeated multiplication:

$$a^n = \underbrace{a \times \cdots \times a}_{n},$$

just as multiplication by a positive integer corresponds to repeated addition:

$$a \times n = \underbrace{a + \cdots + a}_{n}.$$

The _____ is usually shown as a superscript to the right of the base. The exponentiation a^n can be read as: a raised to the n-th power, a raised to the power [of] n or possibly a raised to the _____ [of] n, or more briefly: a to the n-th power or a to the power [of] n, or even more briefly: a to the n.

  a. Exponent
  b. Exponentiating by squaring
  c. Exponential sum
  d. Exponential tree

2. A _____ is one of the basic shapes of geometry: a polygon with three corners or vertices and three sides or edges which are line segments. A _____ with vertices A, B, and C is denoted ABC.

In Euclidean geometry any three non-collinear points determine a unique _____ and a unique plane.

  a. Fuhrmann circle
  b. 1-center problem
  c. Triangle
  d. Kepler triangle

3. In arithmetic and number theory, the _____ or lowest common multiple or smallest common multiple of two integers a and b is the smallest positive integer that is a multiple of both a and b. Since it is a multiple, it can be divided by a and b without a remainder. If either a or b is 0, so that there is no such positive integer, then lc is defined to be zero.
  a. Plus and minus signs
  b. Lowest common denominator
  c. Plus-minus sign
  d. Least common multiple

4. In mathematics, a _____ is a natural number which has exactly two distinct natural number divisors: 1 and itself. An infinitude of _____s exists, as demonstrated by Euclid around 300 BC. The first twenty-five _____s are:

2, 3, 5, 7, 11, 13, 17, 19, 23, 29, 31, 37, 41, 43, 47, 53, 59, 61, 67, 71, 73, 79, 83, 89, 97.

a. Highly composite number
b. Perrin number
c. Prime number
d. Pronic number

5. In number theory, the _____s of a positive integer are the prime numbers that divide into that integer exactly, without leaving a remainder. The process of finding these numbers is called integer factorization, or prime factorization.

For a _____ p of n, the multiplicity of p is the largest exponent a for which p^a divides n.

a. Cunningham chain
b. Gigantic prime
c. Wieferich pair
d. Prime Factor

6. A _____ is a software program that facilitates symbolic mathematics. The core functionality of a CAS is manipulation of mathematical expressions in symbolic form.

The symbolic manipulations supported typically include

- simplification to the smallest possible expression or some standard form, including automatic simplification with assumptions and simplification with constraints
- substitution of symbolic, functors or numeric values for expressions
- change of form of expressions: expanding products and powers, partial and full factorization, rewriting as partial fractions, constraint satisfaction, rewriting trigonometric functions as exponentials, etc.
- partial and total differentiation
- symbolic constrained and unconstrained global optimization
- solution of linear and some non-linear equations over various domains
- solution of some differential and difference equations
- taking some limits
- some indefinite and definite integration, including multidimensional integrals
- integral transforms
- arbitrary-precision numeric operations
- Series operations such as expansion, summation and products
- matrix operations including products, inverses, etc.
- display of mathematical expressions in two-dimensional mathematical form, often using typesetting systems similar to TeX
- add-ons for use in applied mathematics such as physics packages for physical computation
- plotting graphs and parametric plots of functions in two and three dimensions, and animating them
- APIs for linking it on an external program such as a database, or using in a programming language to use the _____
- drawing charts and diagrams
- string manipulation such as matching and searching
- statistical computation
- Theorem proving and verification
- graphic production and editing such as CGI and signal processing as image processing
- sound synthesis

Many also include a programming language, allowing users to implement their own algorithms.

Some _____ s focus on a specific area of application; these are typically developed in academia and are free.

a. 1-center problem
b. 120-cell
c. Computer algebra system
d. 2-3 heap

7. In mathematics, an _____ in the sense of ring theory is a subring $\mathcal{O}$ of a ring R that satisfies the conditions

   1. R is a ring which is a finite-dimensional algebra over the rational number field $\mathbb{Q}$
   2. $\mathcal{O}$ spans R over $\mathbb{Q}$, so that $\mathbb{Q}\mathcal{O} = R$, and
   3. $\mathcal{O}$ is a lattice in R.

The third condition can be stated more accurately, in terms of the extension of scalars of R to the real numbers, embedding R in a real vector space. In less formal terms, additively $\mathcal{O}$ should be a free abelian group generated by a basis for R over $\mathbb{Q}$.

The leading example is the case where R is a number field K and $\mathcal{O}$ is its ring of integers. In algebraic number theory there are examples for any K other than the rational field of proper subrings of the ring of integers that are also _____ s.

   a. Annihilator
   b. Efficiency
   c. Algebraic
   d. Order

8. In algebra and computer programming, when a number or expression is both preceded and followed by a binary operation, a rule is required for which operation should be applied first; this rule is known as an _____ . From the earliest use of mathematical notation, multiplication took precedence over addition, whichever side of a number it appeared on. Thus 3 + 4 × 5 = 5 × 4 + 3 = 23.
   a. Identity element
   b. Order of Operations
   c. Algebraic K-theory
   d. Isomorphism class

9. A vulgar fraction (or common fraction) is a rational number written as one integer (the numerator) divided by a non-zero integer (the denominator).

A vulgar fraction is said to be a _____ if the absolute value of the numerator is less than the absolute value of the denominator--that is, if the absolute value of the entire fraction is less than 1.

   a. 120-cell
   b. 1-center problem
   c. Farey sequence
   d. Proper fraction

10. In mathematics, the _____ of a real number is its numerical value without regard to its sign. So, for example, 3 is the _____ of both 3 and −3.

The _____ of a number a is denoted by | a |.

Generalizations of the _____ for real numbers occur in a wide variety of mathematical settings.

   a. A Mathematical Theory of Communication
   b. Absolute value
   c. Area hyperbolic functions
   d. A chemical equation

11. In the study of metric spaces in mathematics, there are various notions of two metrics on the same underlying space being 'the same', or _____.

In the following, M will denote a non-empty set and d_1 and d_2 will denote two metrics on M.

The two metrics d_1 and d_2 are said to be topologically _____ if they generate the same topology on M.

   a. A chemical equation
   b. A posteriori
   c. A Mathematical Theory of Communication
   d. Equivalent

12. In mathematics, a _____ is a picture of a straight line in which the integers are shown as specially-marked points evenly spaced on the line. Although this image only shows the integers from -9 to 9, the line includes all real numbers, continuing 'forever' in each direction. It is often used as an aid in teaching simple addition and subtraction, especially involving negative numbers.
   a. Real number
   b. Number system
   c. Point plotting
   d. Number line

13. A bar chart or _____ is a chart with rectangular bars with lengths proportional to the values that they represent. Bar charts are used for comparing two or more values. The bars can be horizontally or vertically oriented.

a. 1-center problem
b. 2-3 heap
c. 120-cell
d. Bar graph

14. In mathematics, an _____ is a statement about the relative size or order of two objects, or about whether they are the same or not

- The notation a < b means that a is less than b.
- The notation a > b means that a is greater than b.
- The notation a ≠ b means that a is not equal to b, but does not say that one is bigger than the other or even that they can be compared in size.

In all these cases, a is not equal to b, hence, '_____'.

These relations are known as strict _____

- The notation a ≤ b means that a is less than or equal to b;
- The notation a ≥ b means that a is greater than or equal to b;

An additional use of the notation is to show that one quantity is much greater than another, normally by several orders of magnitude.

- The notation a << b means that a is much less than b.
- The notation a >> b means that a is much greater than b.

If the sense of the _____ is the same for all values of the variables for which its members are defined, then the _____ is called an 'absolute' or 'unconditional' _____. If the sense of an _____ holds only for certain values of the variables involved, but is reversed or destroyed for other values of the variables, it is called a conditional _____.

An _____ may appear unsolvable because it only states whether a number is larger or smaller than another number; but it is possible to apply the same operations for equalities to inequalities. For example, to find x for the _____ 10x > 23 one would divide 23 by 10.

a. A chemical equation
b. A posteriori
c. A Mathematical Theory of Communication
d. Inequality

15. In mathematics, the _____ or least common denominator is the least common multiple of the denominators of a set of vulgar fractions. It is the smallest positive integer that is a multiple of the denominators. For instance, the _____ of

$$\left\{\frac{5}{12}, \frac{11}{18}\right\}$$

is 36 because the least common multiple of 12 and 18 is 36.

   a. The number 0 is even.
   b. Subtrahend
   c. Highest common factor
   d. Lowest common denominator

16. The _____ is a rule which states that when you add or multiply numbers, changing the order doesn't change the result.
   a. Coimage
   b. Semigroupoid
   c. Conditional event algebra
   d. Commutative law

17. A _____ is a device for performing mathematical calculations, distinguished from a computer by having a limited problem solving ability and an interface optimized for interactive calculation rather than programming. _____s can be hardware or software, and mechanical or electronic, and are often built into devices such as PDAs or mobile phones.

Modern electronic _____s are generally small, digital, and usually inexpensive.

   a. Calculator
   b. 120-cell
   c. 1-center problem
   d. 2-3 heap

18. In mathematics, the _____ of a number n is the number that, when added to n, yields zero. The _____ of n is denoted −n. For example, 7 is −7, because 7 + (−7) = 0, and the _____ of −0.3 is 0.3, because −0.3 + 0.3 = 0.
   a. Arity
   b. Associativity
   c. Algebraic structure
   d. Additive inverse

19. Any mathematical statement that contains a variable is a _____.
    a. Convex and concave
    b. Complex Mexican hat wavelet
    c. Classification of the finite simple groups
    d. Variable expression

20. In mathematics, and in particular in abstract algebra, distributivity is a property of binary operations that generalises the _____ law from elementary algebra.
    a. Permutation
    b. Distributive
    c. General linear group
    d. Closure with a twist

21. In mathematics, a _____ for a number x, denoted by $\frac{1}{x}$ or x^{-1}, is a number which when multiplied by x yields the multiplicative identity, 1. The _____ of x is also called the reciprocal of x. The _____ of a fraction p/q is q/p.
    a. Multiplicative inverse
    b. Golden function
    c. Hyperbolic function
    d. Double exponential

22. In mathematics, the multiplicative inverse of a number x, denoted $1/x$ or x^{-1}, is the number which, when multiplied by x, yields 1. The multiplicative inverse of x is also called the _____ of x.
    a. Reciprocal
    b. 2-3 heap
    c. 1-center problem
    d. 120-cell

23. In mathematics, a _____ can mean either an element of the set {1, 2, 3, ...} or an element of the set {0, 1, 2, 3, ...}. The latter is especially preferred in mathematical logic, set theory, and computer science.

    _____s have two main purposes: they can be used for counting, and they can be used for ordering.

    a. Strong partition cardinal
    b. Suslin cardinal
    c. Cardinal numbers
    d. Natural number

24. _____ is the mathematical operation of scaling one number by another. It is one of the four basic operations in elementary arithmetic.

_____ is defined for whole numbers in terms of repeated addition; for example, 4 multiplied by 3 can be calculated by adding 3 copies of 4 together:

$$4 + 4 + 4 = 12.$$

_____ of rational numbers and real numbers is defined by systematic generalization of this basic idea.

   a. The number 0 is even.
   b. Least common multiple
   c. Highest common factor
   d. Multiplication

25. _____ is a quantity expressing the two-dimensional size of a defined part of a surface, typically a region bounded by a closed curve. The term surface _____ refers to the total _____ of the exposed surface of a 3-dimensional solid, such as the sum of the _____s of the exposed sides of a polyhedron. _____ is an important invariant in the differential geometry of surfaces.
   a. Area
   b. A chemical equation
   c. A posteriori
   d. A Mathematical Theory of Communication

26. In mathematics and computer science, _____ (also base-16, hexa or base, of 16. It uses sixteen distinct symbols, most often the symbols 0-9 to represent values zero to nine, and A, B, C, D, E, F (or a through f) to represent values ten to fifteen.

Its primary use is as a human friendly representation of binary coded values, so it is often used in digital electronics and computer engineering.

   a. Tetradecimal
   b. Hexadecimal
   c. Factoradic
   d. Radix

27. _____ is the measurement of vertical distance, but has two meanings in common use. It can either indicate how 'tall' something is, or how 'high up' it is. For example one could say 'That is a tall building', or 'That airplane is high up in the sky'.

a. 1-center problem
b. 2-3 heap
c. 120-cell
d. Height

28. A _____ is a three-dimensional geometric shape that tapers smoothly from a flat, round base to a point called the apex or vertex. More precisely, it is the solid figure bounded by a plane base and the surface formed by the locus of all straight line segments joining the apex to the perimeter of the base. The term '_____' sometimes refers just to the surface of this solid figure, or just to the lateral surface.
   a. Gravity waves
   b. Blocking
   c. Characteristic
   d. Cone

29. In mathematics, a _____ is an algebraic structure consisting of a set together with an operation that combines any two of its elements to form a third element. To qualify as a _____, the set and operation must satisfy a few conditions called _____ axioms, namely associativity, identity and invertibility. While these are familiar from many mathematical structures, such as number systems--for example, the integers endowed with the addition operation form a _____--the formulation of the axioms is detached from the concrete nature of the _____ and its operation.
   a. Characteristic function
   b. Coherence
   c. Group
   d. Derivative algebra

30. _____ is an art form whose medium is sound organized in time. Common elements of _____ are pitch (which governs melody and harmony), rhythm (and its associated concepts tempo, meter, and articulation), dynamics, and the sonic qualities of timbre and texture.

The creation, performance, significance, and even the definition of _____ vary according to culture and social context.

   a. Music
   b. 120-cell
   c. 2-3 heap
   d. 1-center problem

31. A _____, from the French patron, is a type of theme of recurring events of or objects, sometimes referred to as elements of a set. These elements repeat in a predictable manner. It can be a template or model which can be used to generate things or parts of a thing, especially if the things that are created have enough in common for the underlying _____ to be inferred, in which case the things are said to exhibit the unique _____.
   a. 2-3 heap
   b. Pattern
   c. 1-center problem
   d. 120-cell

Chapter 4. Decimals and Real Numbers

1. Exponentiation is a mathematical operation, written a^n, involving two numbers, the base a and the _____ n. When n is a positive integer, exponentiation corresponds to repeated multiplication:

$$a^n = \underbrace{a \times \cdots \times a}_{n},$$

just as multiplication by a positive integer corresponds to repeated addition:

$$a \times n = \underbrace{a + \cdots + a}_{n}.$$

The _____ is usually shown as a superscript to the right of the base. The exponentiation a^n can be read as: a raised to the n-th power, a raised to the power [of] n or possibly a raised to the _____ [of] n, or more briefly: a to the n-th power or a to the power [of] n, or even more briefly: a to the n.

   a. Exponential tree
   b. Exponentiating by squaring
   c. Exponential sum
   d. Exponent

2. A _____ is one of the basic shapes of geometry: a polygon with three corners or vertices and three sides or edges which are line segments. A _____ with vertices A, B, and C is denoted ABC.

In Euclidean geometry any three non-collinear points determine a unique _____ and a unique plane.

   a. Kepler triangle
   b. Fuhrmann circle
   c. 1-center problem
   d. Triangle

3. In a positional numeral system, the decimal separator is a symbol used to mark the boundary between the integral and the fractional parts of a decimal numeral. When used in context of Arabic numerals, terms implying the symbol used are _____ and decimal comma.

The decimal separator is mathematically a radix point.

   a. Hexadecimal
   b. Tetradecimal
   c. Fibonacci coding
   d. Decimal point

Chapter 4. Decimals and Real Numbers

4. _____ is a numeral system in which each position is related to the next by a constant multiplier, a common ratio, called the base or radix of that numeral system.

   a. Negative base
   b. NegaFibonacci coding
   c. Cyrillic numerals
   d. Place value

5. _____ involves reducing the number of significant digits in a number. The result of _____ is a 'shorter' number having fewer non-zero digits yet similar in magnitude. The result is less precise but easier to use.

   a. Hyper operator
   b. Sudan function
   c. Shabakh
   d. Rounding

6. In mathematics, an _____ is a statement about the relative size or order of two objects, or about whether they are the same or not

   - The notation a < b means that a is less than b.
   - The notation a > b means that a is greater than b.
   - The notation a ≠ b means that a is not equal to b, but does not say that one is bigger than the other or even that they can be compared in size.

In all these cases, a is not equal to b, hence, '_____'.

These relations are known as strict _____

   - The notation a ≤ b means that a is less than or equal to b;
   - The notation a ≥ b means that a is greater than or equal to b;

An additional use of the notation is to show that one quantity is much greater than another, normally by several orders of magnitude.

   - The notation a << b means that a is much less than b.
   - The notation a >> b means that a is much greater than b.

If the sense of the _____ is the same for all values of the variables for which its members are defined, then the _____ is called an 'absolute' or 'unconditional' _____. If the sense of an _____ holds only for certain values of the variables involved, but is reversed or destroyed for other values of the variables, it is called a conditional _____.

An _____ may appear unsolvable because it only states whether a number is larger or smaller than another number; but it is possible to apply the same operations for equalities to inequalities. For example, to find x for the _____ 10x > 23 one would divide 23 by 10.

a. A posteriori
b. A chemical equation
c. A Mathematical Theory of Communication
d. Inequality

7. In mathematics, an _____ in the sense of ring theory is a subring $\mathcal{O}$ of a ring R that satisfies the conditions

  1. R is a ring which is a finite-dimensional algebra over the rational number field $\mathbb{Q}$
  2. $\mathcal{O}$ spans R over $\mathbb{Q}$, so that $\mathbb{Q}\mathcal{O} = R$, and
  3. $\mathcal{O}$ is a lattice in R.

The third condition can be stated more accurately, in terms of the extension of scalars of R to the real numbers, embedding R in a real vector space. In less formal terms, additively $\mathcal{O}$ should be a free abelian group generated by a basis for R over $\mathbb{Q}$.

The leading example is the case where R is a number field K and $\mathcal{O}$ is its ring of integers. In algebraic number theory there are examples for any K other than the rational field of proper subrings of the ring of integers that are also _____s.

a. Annihilator
b. Algebraic
c. Efficiency
d. Order

8. A _____ is a software program that facilitates symbolic mathematics. The core functionality of a CAS is manipulation of mathematical expressions in symbolic form.

The symbolic manipulations supported typically include

- simplification to the smallest possible expression or some standard form, including automatic simplification with assumptions and simplification with constraints
- substitution of symbolic, functors or numeric values for expressions
- change of form of expressions: expanding products and powers, partial and full factorization, rewriting as partial fractions, constraint satisfaction, rewriting trigonometric functions as exponentials, etc.
- partial and total differentiation
- symbolic constrained and unconstrained global optimization
- solution of linear and some non-linear equations over various domains
- solution of some differential and difference equations
- taking some limits
- some indefinite and definite integration, including multidimensional integrals
- integral transforms
- arbitrary-precision numeric operations
- Series operations such as expansion, summation and products
- matrix operations including products, inverses, etc.
- display of mathematical expressions in two-dimensional mathematical form, often using typesetting systems similar to TeX
- add-ons for use in applied mathematics such as physics packages for physical computation
- plotting graphs and parametric plots of functions in two and three dimensions, and animating them
- APIs for linking it on an external program such as a database, or using in a programming language to use the _____
- drawing charts and diagrams
- string manipulation such as matching and searching
- statistical computation
- Theorem proving and verification
- graphic production and editing such as CGI and signal processing as image processing
- sound synthesis

Many also include a programming language, allowing users to implement their own algorithms.

Some _____s focus on a specific area of application; these are typically developed in academia and are free.

a. 120-cell
b. Computer algebra system
c. 1-center problem
d. 2-3 heap

9. The _____ is a rule which states that when you add or multiply numbers, changing the order doesn't change the result.

a. Semigroupoid
b. Coimage
c. Conditional event algebra
d. Commutative law

10. Any mathematical statement that contains a variable is a _____.
a. Variable expression
b. Complex Mexican hat wavelet
c. Classification of the finite simple groups
d. Convex and concave

11. _____ is the mathematical operation of scaling one number by another. It is one of the four basic operations in elementary arithmetic.

_____ is defined for whole numbers in terms of repeated addition; for example, 4 multiplied by 3 can be calculated by adding 3 copies of 4 together:

$$4 + 4 + 4 = 12.$$

_____ of rational numbers and real numbers is defined by systematic generalization of this basic idea.

a. Highest common factor
b. The number 0 is even.
c. Least common multiple
d. Multiplication

12. A _____ is a device for performing mathematical calculations, distinguished from a computer by having a limited problem solving ability and an interface optimized for interactive calculation rather than programming. _____s can be hardware or software, and mechanical or electronic, and are often built into devices such as PDAs or mobile phones.

Modern electronic _____s are generally small, digital, and usually inexpensive.

a. 120-cell
b. Calculator
c. 2-3 heap
d. 1-center problem

13. In mathematics, the _____ of a real number is its numerical value without regard to its sign. So, for example, 3 is the _____ of both 3 and −3.

The _____ of a number a is denoted by $|a|$.

Generalizations of the _____ for real numbers occur in a wide variety of mathematical settings.

   a. A chemical equation
   b. A Mathematical Theory of Communication
   c. Absolute value
   d. Area hyperbolic functions

14. In mathematics, the _____ is a term used to describe the number of times one must apply a given operation to an integer before reaching a fixed point.

Usually, this refers to the additive or multiplicative persistence of an integer, which is how often one has to replace the number by the sum or product of its digits until one reaches a single digit. Because the numbers are broken down into their digits, the additive or multiplicative persistence depends on the radix.

   a. Lychrel number
   b. Coprime
   c. Linear congruence theorem
   d. Persistence of a number

15. In algebra and computer programming, when a number or expression is both preceded and followed by a binary operation, a rule is required for which operation should be applied first; this rule is known as an _____ . From the earliest use of mathematical notation, multiplication took precedence over addition, whichever side of a number it appeared on. Thus 3 + 4 × 5 = 5 × 4 + 3 = 23.
   a. Algebraic K-theory
   b. Order of Operations
   c. Isomorphism class
   d. Identity element

16. In statistics, _____ results in values that are limited above or below, similar to but distinct from the concept of statistical censoring.

Usually the values that insurance adjusters receive are either left-truncated, right-censored or both. For example, if policyholders are subject to a policy limit u, then any loss amounts that are actually above u are reported to the insurance company as being exactly u because u is the amount the insurance companies pay.

a. Fixed point iteration
b. Numerical analysis
c. Descriptive research
d. Truncation

17. In mathematics, in the realm of group theory, a group is said to be _____ if it equals its own commutator subgroup if the group has no nontrivial abelian quotients.

The smallest _____ group is the alternating group A_5. More generally, any non-abelian simple group is _____ since the commutator subgroup is a normal subgroup with abelian quotient.

a. Quaternion group
b. Perfect
c. Group of Lie type
d. Free product

18. In mathematics, a _____ of a number x is a number r such that r^2 = x, or, in other words, a number r whose square is x. Every non-negative real number x has a unique non-negative _____, called the principal _____, which is denoted with a radical symbol as $\sqrt{x}$, or, using exponent notation, as $x^{1/2}$. For example, the principal _____ of 9 is 3, denoted $\sqrt{9}$ = 3, because 3^2 = 3 × 3 = 9.

a. Hyperbolic functions
b. Multiplicative inverse
c. Double exponential
d. Square root

19. In vascular plants, the _____ is the organ of a plant body that typically lies below the surface of the soil. This is not always the case, however, since a _____ can also be aerial (that is, growing above the ground) or aerating (that is, growing up above the ground or especially above water.) Furthermore, a stem normally occurring below ground is not exceptional either

a. 120-cell
b. 1-center problem
c. 2-3 heap
d. Root

20. In mathematics, an algebraic group G contains a unique maximal normal solvable subgroup; and this subgroup is closed. Its identity component is called the _____ of G.

a. Barycentric coordinates
b. Radical
c. Block size
d. Composite

21. A _____ is an expression containing a square root.
a. Radical expression
b. Convolution theorem
c. Convolution
d. Controlled Cryptographic Item

22. In mathematics, a _____ can mean either an element of the set {1, 2, 3, ...} (i.e the positive integers) or an element of the set {0, 1, 2, 3, ...} (i.e. the non-negative integers).
a. Whole number
b. Bounded
c. FISH
d. Degrees of freedom

23. In mathematics, a _____ is a number which can be expressed as a ratio of two integers. Non-integer _____s are usually written as the vulgar fraction $\frac{a}{b}$, where b is not zero. a is called the numerator, and b the denominator.
a. Minkowski distance
b. Tally marks
c. Pre-algebra
d. Rational number

24. In mathematics, a _____ is a picture of a straight line in which the integers are shown as specially-marked points evenly spaced on the line. Although this image only shows the integers from -9 to 9, the line includes all real numbers, continuing 'forever' in each direction. It is often used as an aid in teaching simple addition and subtraction, especially involving negative numbers.
a. Real number
b. Point plotting
c. Number line
d. Number system

Chapter 4. Decimals and Real Numbers

25. In mathematics, the _____s may be described informally in several different ways. The _____s include both rational numbers, such as 42 and −23/129, and irrational numbers, such as pi and the square root of two; or, a _____ can be given by an infinite decimal representation, such as 2.4871773339...., where the digits continue in some way; or, the _____s may be thought of as points on an infinitely long number line.

These descriptions of the _____s, while intuitively accessible, are not sufficiently rigorous for the purposes of pure mathematics.

   a. Tally marks
   b. Minkowski distance
   c. Pre-algebra
   d. Real number

26. A bar chart or _____ is a chart with rectangular bars with lengths proportional to the values that they represent. Bar charts are used for comparing two or more values. The bars can be horizontally or vertically oriented.
   a. 120-cell
   b. 2-3 heap
   c. 1-center problem
   d. Bar graph

27. In mathematics, an inequality is a statement about the relative size or order of two objects. For example 14 > 10, or 14 is _____ 10. The notation a > b means that a is _____ b and 'a' would be to the right of 'b' on a number line.
   a. Cauchy-Schwarz inequality
   b. FKG inequality
   c. Greater than
   d. Minkowski inequality

28. In mathematics, and in particular in abstract algebra, distributivity is a property of binary operations that generalises the _____ law from elementary algebra.
   a. Permutation
   b. Closure with a twist
   c. Distributive
   d. General linear group

Chapter 4. Decimals and Real Numbers

29. In mathematics, a _____ is an algebraic structure consisting of a set together with an operation that combines any two of its elements to form a third element. To qualify as a _____, the set and operation must satisfy a few conditions called _____ axioms, namely associativity, identity and invertibility. While these are familiar from many mathematical structures, such as number systems--for example, the integers endowed with the addition operation form a _____--the formulation of the axioms is detached from the concrete nature of the _____ and its operation.

   a. Group
   b. Derivative algebra
   c. Characteristic function
   d. Coherence

30. In mathematics, a _____ is a constant multiplicative factor of a certain object. For example, in the expression $9x^2$, the _____ of x^2 is 9.

The object can be such things as a variable, a vector, a function, etc.

   a. Fibonacci polynomials
   b. Multivariate division algorithm
   c. Coefficient
   d. Stability radius

Chapter 5. Variable Expressions

1. Exponentiation is a mathematical operation, written a^n, involving two numbers, the base a and the _____ n. When n is a positive integer, exponentiation corresponds to repeated multiplication:

$$a^n = \underbrace{a \times \cdots \times a}_{n},$$

just as multiplication by a positive integer corresponds to repeated addition:

$$a \times n = \underbrace{a + \cdots + a}_{n}.$$

The _____ is usually shown as a superscript to the right of the base. The exponentiation a^n can be read as: a raised to the n-th power, a raised to the power [of] n or possibly a raised to the _____ [of] n, or more briefly: a to the n-th power or a to the power [of] n, or even more briefly: a to the n.

   a. Exponent
   b. Exponential tree
   c. Exponential sum
   d. Exponentiating by squaring

2. A _____ is one of the basic shapes of geometry: a polygon with three corners or vertices and three sides or edges which are line segments. A _____ with vertices A, B, and C is denoted ABC.

In Euclidean geometry any three non-collinear points determine a unique _____ and a unique plane.

   a. Fuhrmann circle
   b. 1-center problem
   c. Kepler triangle
   d. Triangle

3. In mathematics, _____ is a property that a binary operation can have. It means that, within an expression containing two or more of the same associative operators in a row, the order that the operations are performed does not matter as long as the sequence of the operands is not changed. That is, rearranging the parentheses in such an expression will not change its value.
   a. Idempotence
   b. Algebraically closed
   c. Unital
   d. Associativity

4. The _____ is a rule which states that when you add or multiply numbers, changing the order doesn't change the result.

   a. Semigroupoid
   b. Commutative law
   c. Conditional event algebra
   d. Coimage

5. In mathematics, the _____ of a number n is the number that, when added to n, yields zero. The _____ of n is denoted −n. For example, 7 is −7, because 7 + (−7) = 0, and the _____ of −0.3 is 0.3, because −0.3 + 0.3 = 0.

   a. Associativity
   b. Additive inverse
   c. Algebraic structure
   d. Arity

6. _____ is the mathematical operation of scaling one number by another. It is one of the four basic operations in elementary arithmetic.

   _____ is defined for whole numbers in terms of repeated addition; for example, 4 multiplied by 3 can be calculated by adding 3 copies of 4 together:

   $$4 + 4 + 4 = 12.$$

   _____ of rational numbers and real numbers is defined by systematic generalization of this basic idea.

   a. The number 0 is even.
   b. Highest common factor
   c. Least common multiple
   d. Multiplication

7. In mathematics, the _____s may be described informally in several different ways. The _____s include both rational numbers, such as 42 and −23/129, and irrational numbers, such as pi and the square root of two; or, a _____ can be given by an infinite decimal representation, such as 2.4871773339...., where the digits continue in some way; or, the _____s may be thought of as points on an infinitely long number line.

These descriptions of the _____s, while intuitively accessible, are not sufficiently rigorous for the purposes of pure mathematics.

a. Tally marks
b. Pre-algebra
c. Minkowski distance
d. Real number

8. In mathematics, a _____ for a number x, denoted by $1/x$ or x^{-1}, is a number which when multiplied by x yields the multiplicative identity, 1. The _____ of x is also called the reciprocal of x. The _____ of a fraction p/q is q/p.
   a. Double exponential
   b. Hyperbolic function
   c. Golden function
   d. Multiplicative inverse

9. In mathematics, an _____ in the sense of ring theory is a subring $\mathcal{O}$ of a ring R that satisfies the conditions

   1. R is a ring which is a finite-dimensional algebra over the rational number field $\mathbb{Q}$
   2. $\mathcal{O}$ spans R over $\mathbb{Q}$, so that $\mathbb{Q}\mathcal{O} = R$, and
   3. $\mathcal{O}$ is a lattice in R.

The third condition can be stated more accurately, in terms of the extension of scalars of R to the real numbers, embedding R in a real vector space. In less formal terms, additively $\mathcal{O}$ should be a free abelian group generated by a basis for R over $\mathbb{Q}$.

The leading example is the case where R is a number field K and $\mathcal{O}$ is its ring of integers. In algebraic number theory there are examples for any K other than the rational field of proper subrings of the ring of integers that are also _____s.

   a. Order
   b. Algebraic
   c. Annihilator
   d. Efficiency

10. In algebra and computer programming, when a number or expression is both preceded and followed by a binary operation, a rule is required for which operation should be applied first; this rule is known as an _____ . From the earliest use of mathematical notation, multiplication took precedence over addition, whichever side of a number it appeared on. Thus 3 + 4 × 5 = 5 × 4 + 3 = 23.

a. Identity element
b. Algebraic K-theory
c. Isomorphism class
d. Order of Operations

11. In mathematics, the multiplicative inverse of a number x, denoted 1/x or x^{-1}, is the number which, when multiplied by x, yields 1. The multiplicative inverse of x is also called the _____ of x.

a. Reciprocal
b. 1-center problem
c. 2-3 heap
d. 120-cell

12. Any mathematical statement that contains a variable is a _____.

a. Complex Mexican hat wavelet
b. Classification of the finite simple groups
c. Convex and concave
d. Variable expression

13. In mathematics, the _____ of a real number is its numerical value without regard to its sign. So, for example, 3 is the _____ of both 3 and −3.

The _____ of a number a is denoted by $|a|$.

Generalizations of the _____ for real numbers occur in a wide variety of mathematical settings.

a. A Mathematical Theory of Communication
b. A chemical equation
c. Area hyperbolic functions
d. Absolute value

14. In mathematics, and in particular in abstract algebra, distributivity is a property of binary operations that generalises the _____ law from elementary algebra.

a. Closure with a twist
b. Distributive
c. General linear group
d. Permutation

Chapter 5. Variable Expressions

15. In mathematics, a _____ is a constant multiplicative factor of a certain object. For example, in the expression $9x^2$, the _____ of x^2 is 9.

The object can be such things as a variable, a vector, a function, etc.

   a. Stability radius
   b. Coefficient
   c. Fibonacci polynomials
   d. Multivariate division algorithm

16. In mathematics, the _____ of a polynomial is the term of degree 0. For example, in the polynomial

   $X^3 + 2X + 3$

over the variable X, the _____ is 3. Here, the _____ is given by a numeral, but it may also be specified by a letter that is a parameter rather than a variable, as in the polynomial

   $ax^2 + bx + c,$

in the variable x, where a, b, and c are parameters so that c is the _____.

   a. Sheffer sequence
   b. Stability radius
   c. Jacobian conjecture
   d. Constant term

17. In elementary algebra, a _____ is a polynomial with two terms: the sum of two monomials. It is the simplest kind of polynomial except for a monomial.

The _____ $a^2 - b^2$ can be factored as the product of two other _____s:

   $a^2 - b^2$.

The product of a pair of linear _____s a x + b and c x + d is:

   2 +x + bd.

A _____ raised to the nth power, represented as

n

can be expanded by means of the _____ theorem or, equivalently, using Pascal's triangle.

   a. Rational root theorem
   b. Binomial
   c. Cylindrical algebraic decomposition
   d. Real structure

18. In mathematics, the word _____ means two different things in the context of polynomials:

   - The first meaning is a product of powers of variables, or formally any value obtained from 1 by finitely many multiplications by a variable. If only a single variable x is considered this means that any _____ is either 1 or a power x^n of x, with n a positive integer. If several variables are considered, say, x, y, z, then each can be given an exponent, so that any _____ is of the form $x^a y^b z^c$ with a,b,c nonnegative integers.
   - The second meaning of _____ includes _____s in the first sense, but also allows multiplication by any constant, so that − $7x^5$ and $4yz^{13}$ are also considered to be _____s.

With either definition, the set of _____s is a subset of all polynomials that is closed under multiplication.

   a. Power sum symmetric polynomial
   b. Diagonal form
   c. Homogeneous polynomial
   d. Monomial

19. In mathematics, a _____ is an expression constructed from variables and constants, using the operations of addition, subtraction, multiplication, and constant non-negative whole number exponents. For example, $x^2 − 4x + 7$ is a _____, but $x^2 − 4/x + 7x^{3/2}$ is not, because its second term involves division by the variable x and also because its third term contains an exponent that is not a whole number.

_____s are one of the most important concepts in algebra and throughout mathematics and science.

   a. Group extension
   b. Semifield
   c. Coimage
   d. Polynomial

Chapter 5. Variable Expressions

20. In elementary algebra, a _____ is a polynomial consisting of three terms; in other words, a _____ is the sum of three monomials. It can be factored using simple steps

In linguistics, a _____ is a fixed expression which is made from three words; e.g. 'lights, camera, action', 'signed, sealed, delivered'.

   a. Relation algebra
   b. Recurrence relation
   c. Symmetric difference
   d. Trinomial

21. In economics, business, retail, and accounting, a _____ is the value of money that has been used up to produce something, and hence is not available for use anymore. In business, the _____ may be one of acquisition, in which case the amount of money expended to acquire it is counted as _____. In this case, money is the input that is gone in order to acquire the thing.
   a. 1-center problem
   b. 120-cell
   c. Cost
   d. 2-3 heap

22. A _____ is a software program that facilitates symbolic mathematics. The core functionality of a CAS is manipulation of mathematical expressions in symbolic form.

The symbolic manipulations supported typically include

- simplification to the smallest possible expression or some standard form, including automatic simplification with assumptions and simplification with constraints
- substitution of symbolic, functors or numeric values for expressions
- change of form of expressions: expanding products and powers, partial and full factorization, rewriting as partial fractions, constraint satisfaction, rewriting trigonometric functions as exponentials, etc.
- partial and total differentiation
- symbolic constrained and unconstrained global optimization
- solution of linear and some non-linear equations over various domains
- solution of some differential and difference equations
- taking some limits
- some indefinite and definite integration, including multidimensional integrals
- integral transforms
- arbitrary-precision numeric operations
- Series operations such as expansion, summation and products
- matrix operations including products, inverses, etc.
- display of mathematical expressions in two-dimensional mathematical form, often using typesetting systems similar to TeX
- add-ons for use in applied mathematics such as physics packages for physical computation
- plotting graphs and parametric plots of functions in two and three dimensions, and animating them
- APIs for linking it on an external program such as a database, or using in a programming language to use the _____
- drawing charts and diagrams
- string manipulation such as matching and searching
- statistical computation
- Theorem proving and verification
- graphic production and editing such as CGI and signal processing as image processing
- sound synthesis

Many also include a programming language, allowing users to implement their own algorithms.

Some _____s focus on a specific area of application; these are typically developed in academia and are free.

a. 1-center problem
b. 120-cell
c. 2-3 heap
d. Computer algebra system

23. In mathematics and computer science, _____ (also base-16, hexa or base, of 16. It uses sixteen distinct symbols, most often the symbols 0-9 to represent values zero to nine, and A, B, C, D, E, F (or a through f) to represent values ten to fifteen.

Its primary use is as a human friendly representation of binary coded values, so it is often used in digital electronics and computer engineering.

   a. Tetradecimal
   b. Hexadecimal
   c. Factoradic
   d. Radix

24. A _____ is a device for performing mathematical calculations, distinguished from a computer by having a limited problem solving ability and an interface optimized for interactive calculation rather than programming. _____s can be hardware or software, and mechanical or electronic, and are often built into devices such as PDAs or mobile phones.

Modern electronic _____s are generally small, digital, and usually inexpensive.

   a. 120-cell
   b. 1-center problem
   c. 2-3 heap
   d. Calculator

25. A _____ is a three-dimensional geometric shape that tapers smoothly from a flat, round base to a point called the apex or vertex. More precisely, it is the solid figure bounded by a plane base and the surface formed by the locus of all straight line segments joining the apex to the perimeter of the base. The term '_____' sometimes refers just to the surface of this solid figure, or just to the lateral surface.
   a. Blocking
   b. Gravity waves
   c. Characteristic
   d. Cone

26. In mathematics, a _____ is a total order on the set of all monomials satisfying two additional properties.

   1. If u < v and w is any other monomial, then uw<vw. In other words, the ordering respects multiplication.
   2. The ordering is a well ordering

Most _____s impose an ordering on the indeterminates, but differ in their exact details. Some important examples of _____s include:

- Lexicographic order orders according to the highest power of the most significant indeterminate, using less significant indeterminates to break ties.

- Reverse lexicographic order orders according to the lowest power of the least significant indeterminate, using more significant indeterminates to break ties.

- Graded lexicographic order orders by total degree first, then breaks ties using lexicographic order.

- Graded reverse lexicographic order orders by total degree first, then breaks ties using reverse lexicographic order.

- An elimination order guarantees that a monomial involving any of a set of indeterminates will always be greater than a monomial not involving any of them.

- A product order orders one set of indeterminates using one _____, then breaks ties using a different order on a second set.

- Weight orders treat the powers of indeterminates as a vector and orders according to the dot product with a weight vector.

All _____s can be constructed as product orders of weight orders

For example, consider the monomials xy^2z, z^2, x^3, and x^2z^2. Using the indeterminate order $x > y > z$, here's how some of the _____s above would order these four monomials:

- Lex: $x^3 > x^2z^2 > xy^2z > z^2$
- Grlex: $x^2z^2 > xy^2z > x^3 > z^2$
- Grevlex: $xy^2z > x^2z^2 > x^3 > z^2$

Monomial orderings are most commonly used with Groebner bases and multivariate division, and different orders can led to different results. For example, grevlex has a reputation for producing relatively small Groebner bases, while elimination orders can be used with the same algorithms to solve systems of polynomial equations by eliminating variables.

a. Partially ordered set
b. Comparability graph
c. Non-increasing sequence
d. Monomial Order

Chapter 5. Variable Expressions

27. _____, also sometimes known as standard form or as exponential notation, is a way of writing numbers that accommodates values too large or small to be conveniently written in standard decimal notation. _____ has a number of useful properties and is often favored by scientists, mathematicians and engineers, who work with such numbers.

In _____, numbers are written in the form:

$$a \times 10^b$$

   a. Leading zero
   b. 1-center problem
   c. Radix point
   d. Scientific notation

28. In mathematics, a _____ is the end result of a division problem. It can also be expressed as the number of times the divisor divides into the dividend.
   a. Marginal cost
   b. Limiting
   c. Quotient
   d. Notation

29. A _____, from the French patron, is a type of theme of recurring events of or objects, sometimes referred to as elements of a set. These elements repeat in a predictable manner. It can be a template or model which can be used to generate things or parts of a thing, especially if the things that are created have enough in common for the underlying _____ to be inferred, in which case the things are said to exhibit the unique _____.
   a. 120-cell
   b. Pattern
   c. 1-center problem
   d. 2-3 heap

30. In mathematics, a _____ is an algebraic structure consisting of a set together with an operation that combines any two of its elements to form a third element. To qualify as a _____, the set and operation must satisfy a few conditions called _____ axioms, namely associativity, identity and invertibility. While these are familiar from many mathematical structures, such as number systems--for example, the integers endowed with the addition operation form a _____--the formulation of the axioms is detached from the concrete nature of the _____ and its operation.
   a. Coherence
   b. Characteristic function
   c. Group
   d. Derivative algebra

1. Exponentiation is a mathematical operation, written a^n, involving two numbers, the base a and the _____ n. When n is a positive integer, exponentiation corresponds to repeated multiplication:

$$a^n = \underbrace{a \times \cdots \times a}_{n},$$

just as multiplication by a positive integer corresponds to repeated addition:

$$a \times n = \underbrace{a + \cdots + a}_{n}.$$

The _____ is usually shown as a superscript to the right of the base. The exponentiation a^n can be read as: a raised to the n-th power, a raised to the power [of] n or possibly a raised to the _____ [of] n, or more briefly: a to the n-th power or a to the power [of] n, or even more briefly: a to the n.

   a. Exponential sum
   b. Exponentiating by squaring
   c. Exponent
   d. Exponential tree

2. A _____ is one of the basic shapes of geometry: a polygon with three corners or vertices and three sides or edges which are line segments. A _____ with vertices A, B, and C is denoted ABC.

In Euclidean geometry any three non-collinear points determine a unique _____ and a unique plane.

   a. Triangle
   b. 1-center problem
   c. Fuhrmann circle
   d. Kepler triangle

3. _____ is the mathematical operation of scaling one number by another. It is one of the four basic operations in elementary arithmetic.

_____ is defined for whole numbers in terms of repeated addition; for example, 4 multiplied by 3 can be calculated by adding 3 copies of 4 together:

$$4 + 4 + 4 = 12.$$

_____ of rational numbers and real numbers is defined by systematic generalization of this basic idea.

a. Multiplication
b. Highest common factor
c. The number 0 is even.
d. Least common multiple

4. In mathematics, an _____ in the sense of ring theory is a subring $\mathcal{O}$ of a ring R that satisfies the conditions

   1. R is a ring which is a finite-dimensional algebra over the rational number field $\mathbb{Q}$
   2. $\mathcal{O}$ spans R over $\mathbb{Q}$, so that $\mathbb{Q}\mathcal{O} = R$, and
   3. $\mathcal{O}$ is a lattice in R.

The third condition can be stated more accurately, in terms of the extension of scalars of R to the real numbers, embedding R in a real vector space. In less formal terms, additively $\mathcal{O}$ should be a free abelian group generated by a basis for R over $\mathbb{Q}$.

The leading example is the case where R is a number field K and $\mathcal{O}$ is its ring of integers. In algebraic number theory there are examples for any K other than the rational field of proper subrings of the ring of integers that are also _____ s.

a. Annihilator
b. Efficiency
c. Order
d. Algebraic

5. In algebra and computer programming, when a number or expression is both preceded and followed by a binary operation, a rule is required for which operation should be applied first; this rule is known as an _____ . From the earliest use of mathematical notation, multiplication took precedence over addition, whichever side of a number it appeared on. Thus 3 + 4 × 5 = 5 × 4 + 3 = 23.
a. Identity element
b. Order of Operations
c. Isomorphism class
d. Algebraic K-theory

6. A _____ is a software program that facilitates symbolic mathematics. The core functionality of a CAS is manipulation of mathematical expressions in symbolic form.

The symbolic manipulations supported typically include

- simplification to the smallest possible expression or some standard form, including automatic simplification with assumptions and simplification with constraints
- substitution of symbolic, functors or numeric values for expressions
- change of form of expressions: expanding products and powers, partial and full factorization, rewriting as partial fractions, constraint satisfaction, rewriting trigonometric functions as exponentials, etc.
- partial and total differentiation
- symbolic constrained and unconstrained global optimization
- solution of linear and some non-linear equations over various domains
- solution of some differential and difference equations
- taking some limits
- some indefinite and definite integration, including multidimensional integrals
- integral transforms
- arbitrary-precision numeric operations
- Series operations such as expansion, summation and products
- matrix operations including products, inverses, etc.
- display of mathematical expressions in two-dimensional mathematical form, often using typesetting systems similar to TeX
- add-ons for use in applied mathematics such as physics packages for physical computation
- plotting graphs and parametric plots of functions in two and three dimensions, and animating them
- APIs for linking it on an external program such as a database, or using in a programming language to use the _____
- drawing charts and diagrams
- string manipulation such as matching and searching
- statistical computation
- Theorem proving and verification
- graphic production and editing such as CGI and signal processing as image processing
- sound synthesis

Many also include a programming language, allowing users to implement their own algorithms.

Some _____s focus on a specific area of application; these are typically developed in academia and are free.

a. 120-cell
b. 1-center problem
c. 2-3 heap
d. Computer algebra system

Chapter 6. First-Degree Equations

7. A _____ is a device for performing mathematical calculations, distinguished from a computer by having a limited problem solving ability and an interface optimized for interactive calculation rather than programming. _____s can be hardware or software, and mechanical or electronic, and are often built into devices such as PDAs or mobile phones.

Modern electronic _____s are generally small, digital, and usually inexpensive.

   a. Calculator
   b. 2-3 heap
   c. 120-cell
   d. 1-center problem

8. In mathematics, and in particular in abstract algebra, distributivity is a property of binary operations that generalises the _____ law from elementary algebra.
   a. Permutation
   b. General linear group
   c. Closure with a twist
   d. Distributive

9. In mathematics, the term _____ has several different important meanings:

   - An _____ is an equality that remains true regardless of the values of any variables that appear within it, to distinguish it from an equality which is true under more particular conditions. For this, the 'triple bar' symbol ≡ is sometimes used.
   - In algebra, an _____ or _____ element of a set S with a binary operation Â· is an element e that, when combined with any element x of S, produces that same x. That is, eÂ·x = xÂ·e = x for all x in S.
     - The _____ function from a set S to itself, often denoted id or id$_S$, s the function such that i = x for all x in S. This function serves as the _____ element in the set of all functions from S to itself with respect to function composition.
     - In linear algebra, the _____ matrix of size n is the n-by-n square matrix with ones on the main diagonal and zeros elsewhere. This matrix serves as the _____ with respect to matrix multiplication.

A common example of the first meaning is the trigonometric _____

$$\sin^2 \theta + \cos^2 \theta = 1$$

which is true for all real values of θ, as opposed to

$$\cos \theta = 1,$$

which is true only for some values of θ, not all. For example, the latter equation is true when $\theta = 0$, false when $\theta = 2$

The concepts of 'additive _____' and 'multiplicative _____' are central to the Peano axioms. The number 0 is the 'additive _____' for integers, real numbers, and complex numbers. For the real numbers, for all $a \in \mathbb{R}$,

$$0 + a = a,$$

$$a + 0 = a, \text{ and}$$

$$0 + 0 = 0.$$

Similarly, The number 1 is the 'multiplicative _____' for integers, real numbers, and complex numbers.

a. Action
b. Intersection
c. ARIA
d. Identity

10. _____ is the study of geometry using the principles of algebra. That the algebra of the real numbers can be employed to yield results about the linear continuum of geometry relies on the Cantor-Dedekind axiom. Usually the Cartesian coordinate system is applied to manipulate equations for planes, straight lines, and squares, often in two and sometimes in three dimensions of measurement.
   a. Analytic geometry
   b. Angular eccentricity
   c. Ambient space
   d. Axis-aligned object

11. _____ is a part of mathematics concerned with questions of size, shape, and relative position of figures and with properties of space. _____ is one of the oldest sciences. Initially a body of practical knowledge concerning lengths, areas, and volumes, in the third century BC _____ was put into an axiomatic form by Euclid, whose treatment--Euclidean _____--set a standard for many centuries to follow.
   a. 120-cell
   b. 1-center problem
   c. 2-3 heap
   d. Geometry

Chapter 6. First-Degree Equations

12. In mathematics, an _____ is a statement about the relative size or order of two objects, or about whether they are the same or not

    - The notation a < b means that a is less than b.
    - The notation a > b means that a is greater than b.
    - The notation a ≠ b means that a is not equal to b, but does not say that one is bigger than the other or even that they can be compared in size.

In all these cases, a is not equal to b, hence, '_____'.

These relations are known as strict _____

    - The notation a ≤ b means that a is less than or equal to b;
    - The notation a ≥ b means that a is greater than or equal to b;

An additional use of the notation is to show that one quantity is much greater than another, normally by several orders of magnitude.

    - The notation a << b means that a is much less than b.
    - The notation a >> b means that a is much greater than b.

If the sense of the _____ is the same for all values of the variables for which its members are defined, then the _____ is called an 'absolute' or 'unconditional' _____. If the sense of an _____ holds only for certain values of the variables involved, but is reversed or destroyed for other values of the variables, it is called a conditional _____.

An _____ may appear unsolvable because it only states whether a number is larger or smaller than another number; but it is possible to apply the same operations for equalities to inequalities. For example, to find x for the _____ 10x > 23 one would divide 23 by 10.

  a. A Mathematical Theory of Communication
  b. A chemical equation
  c. A posteriori
  d. Inequality

13. In quantum field theory and statistical mechanics in the thermodynamic limit, a system with a global symmetry can have more than one phase. For parameters where the symmetry is spontaneously broken, the system is said to be _____. When the global symmetry is unbroken the system is disordered.

a. Einstein relation
b. Ursell function
c. Ordered
d. Isoenthalpic-isobaric ensemble

14. In mathematics, an _____ is a collection of objects having two coordinates (or entries or projections), such that one can always uniquely determine the object, which is the first coordinate (or first entry or left projection) of the pair as well as the second coordinate (or second entry or right projection.) If the first coordinate is a and the second is b, the usual notation for an _____ is (a, b.) The pair is 'ordered' in that (a, b) differs from (b, a) unless a = b.
 a. A chemical equation
 b. A posteriori
 c. A Mathematical Theory of Communication
 d. Ordered pair

15. In mathematics, the _____ of a Euclidean space is a special point, usually denoted by the letter O, used as a fixed point of reference for the geometry of the surrounding space. In a Cartesian coordinate system, the _____ is the point where the axes of the system intersect. In Euclidean geometry, the _____ may be chosen freely as any convenient point of reference.
 a. Interval
 b. OMAC
 c. Autonomous system
 d. Origin

16. In mathematics, a _____ is, informally, an infinitely vast and infinitely thin sheet. _____s may be thought of as objects in some higher dimensional space, or they may be considered without any outside space, as in the setting of Euclidean geometry
 a. Plane
 b. Bandwidth
 c. Group
 d. Blocking

17. A _____ is is a graphical technique for presenting a data set drawn by hand or produced by a mechanical or electronic plotter. It is a graph depicting the relationship between two or more variables used, for instance, in visualising scientific data.

_____s play an important role in statistics and data analysis.

a. Plot
b. Dini
c. C-35
d. Lattice

18. A _____ consists of one quarter of the coordinate plane.
a. Quadrant
b. 120-cell
c. 2-3 heap
d. 1-center problem

19. A bar chart or _____ is a chart with rectangular bars with lengths proportional to the values that they represent. Bar charts are used for comparing two or more values. The bars can be horizontally or vertically oriented.
a. 120-cell
b. 2-3 heap
c. 1-center problem
d. Bar graph

20. In set theory and its applications throughout mathematics, a _____ is a collection of sets that can be unambiguously defined by a property that all its members share. The precise definition of '_____' depends on foundational context. In work on ZF set theory, the notion of _____ is informal, whereas other set theories, such as NBG set theory, axiomatize the notion of '_____'.
a. Coherence
b. Filter
c. Class
d. Congruent

21. In mathematics, a _____ is a picture of a straight line in which the integers are shown as specially-marked points evenly spaced on the line. Although this image only shows the integers from -9 to 9, the line includes all real numbers, continuing 'forever' in each direction. It is often used as an aid in teaching simple addition and subtraction, especially involving negative numbers.
a. Number line
b. Point plotting
c. Real number
d. Number system

22. The _____ is one of the coordinates of a point in a two or three-dimensional cartesian coordinate system, equal to the distance of a point from the y-axis in a 2D system, or from the plane of y and z axes in a 3D system, measured along a line parallel to the x axis.

a. 1-center problem
b. X-coordinate
c. 2-3 heap
d. 120-cell

23. The _____ is the distance between a point and an axis in the Cartesian Coordinate System.

a. 1-center problem
b. 2-3 heap
c. 120-cell
d. Y-coordinate

24. A _____ is a 2D geometric symbolic representation of information according to some visualization technique. Sometimes, the technique uses a 3D visualization which is then projected onto the 2D surface. The word graph is sometimes used as a synonym for _____.

a. 120-cell
b. 1-center problem
c. 2-3 heap
d. Diagram

25. A _____ is an algebraic equation in which each term is either a constant or the product of a constant and a single variable. _____s can have one, two, three or more variables.

_____s occur with great regularity in applied mathematics.

a. Quartic equation
b. Quadratic equation
c. Difference of two squares
d. Linear equation

26. In mathematics, the _____ is an approach to finding a particular solution to certain inhomogeneous ordinary differential equations and recurrence relations. It is closely related to the annihilator method, but instead of using a particular kind of differential operator in order to find the best possible form of the particular solution, a 'guess' is made as to the appropriate form, which is then tested by differentiating the resulting equation. In this sense, the _____ is less formal but more intuitive than the annihilator method.

a. Phase line
b. Linear differential equation
c. Differential algebraic equations
d. Method of undetermined coefficients

27. In information theory, a _____ is a function mapping an alphabet to non-negative real numbers, satisfying a generalization of Kraft's inequality. A _____ page, a type of character encoding table, is one such _____.
   a. Code
   b. Deterministic encryption
   c. Link encryption
   d. File Camouflage

28. In geometry, two sets of points are called _____ if one can be transformed into the other by an isometry. Less formally, two figures are _____ if they have the same shape and size, but are in different positions.

In a Euclidean system, congruence is fundamental; it is the counterpart of equality for numbers.

   a. Germ
   b. Congruent
   c. Gamma test
   d. Function

29. In mathematics, a _____ is an algebraic structure consisting of a set together with an operation that combines any two of its elements to form a third element. To qualify as a _____, the set and operation must satisfy a few conditions called _____ axioms, namely associativity, identity and invertibility. While these are familiar from many mathematical structures, such as number systems--for example, the integers endowed with the addition operation form a _____ --the formulation of the axioms is detached from the concrete nature of the _____ and its operation.
   a. Group
   b. Characteristic function
   c. Derivative algebra
   d. Coherence

30. In mathematics the concept of a _____ generalizes notions such as 'length', 'area', and 'volume'. Informally, given some base set, a '_____' is any consistent assignment of 'sizes' to the subsets of the base set. Depending on the application, the 'size' of a subset may be interpreted as its physical size, the amount of something that lies within the subset, or the probability that some random process will yield a result within the subset.

a. Cusp
b. Congruent
c. Measure
d. Lattice

31. In mathematics, _____ is a system of arithmetic for integers, where numbers 'wrap around' after they reach a certain value -- the modulus. _____ was introduced by Carl Friedrich Gauss in his book Disquisitiones Arithmeticae, published in 1801.

A familiar use of _____ is its use in the 24-hour clock: the arithmetic of time-keeping in which the day runs from midnight to midnight and is divided into 24 hours, numbered from 0 to 23.

a. Discrete logarithm
b. Multiplicative group of integers modulo n
c. Residue number system
d. Modular arithmetic

32. The _____ is a barcode symbology, that is widely used in the United States and Canada for tracking trade items in stores. In the _____-A barcode, each digit is represented by a seven-bit sequence, encoded by a series of alternating bars and spaces. Guard bars, shown in green, separate the two groups of six digits.

The _____ encodes 12 decimal digits as SLLLLLLMRRRRRRE, where S and E are the bit pattern 101, M is the bit pattern 01010, and each L and R are digits, each one represented by a seven-bit code.

a. A chemical equation
b. A posteriori
c. A Mathematical Theory of Communication
d. Universal Product Code

33. The word _____ is the Latin ablative of modulus which itself means 'a small measure.' It was introduced into mathematics in the book Disquisitiones Arithmeticae by Carl Friedrich Gauss in 1801. Ever since, however, '_____' has gained many meanings, some exact and some imprecise.

- (This usage is from Gauss's book.) Given the integers a, b and n, the expression a ≡ b (mod n) means that a − b is a multiple of n, or equivalently, a and b both leave the same remainder when divided by n. For more details, see modular arithmetic.

- In computing, given two numbers (either integer or real), a and n, a _____ n is the remainder after numerical division of a by n, under certain constraints. See _____ operation.

a. Per mil
b. Quotition
c. Predictor-corrector method
d. Modulo

1. Exponentiation is a mathematical operation, written a^n, involving two numbers, the base a and the _____ n. When n is a positive integer, exponentiation corresponds to repeated multiplication:

$$a^n = \underbrace{a \times \cdots \times a}_{n},$$

just as multiplication by a positive integer corresponds to repeated addition:

$$a \times n = \underbrace{a + \cdots + a}_{n}.$$

The _____ is usually shown as a superscript to the right of the base. The exponentiation a^n can be read as: a raised to the n-th power, a raised to the power [of] n or possibly a raised to the _____ [of] n, or more briefly: a to the n-th power or a to the power [of] n, or even more briefly: a to the n.

   a. Exponentiating by squaring
   b. Exponential tree
   c. Exponential sum
   d. Exponent

2. A _____ is one of the basic shapes of geometry: a polygon with three corners or vertices and three sides or edges which are line segments. A _____ with vertices A, B, and C is denoted ABC.

In Euclidean geometry any three non-collinear points determine a unique _____ and a unique plane.

   a. 1-center problem
   b. Kepler triangle
   c. Fuhrmann circle
   d. Triangle

3. In mathematics the concept of a _____ generalizes notions such as 'length', 'area', and 'volume'. Informally, given some base set, a '_____' is any consistent assignment of 'sizes' to the subsets of the base set. Depending on the application, the 'size' of a subset may be interpreted as its physical size, the amount of something that lies within the subset, or the probability that some random process will yield a result within the subset.
   a. Measure
   b. Cusp
   c. Lattice
   d. Congruent

Chapter 7. Measurement and Proportion

4. The _____ is a decimalised system of measurement. It exists in several variations, with different choices of base units, though the choice of base units does not affect its day-to-day use. Over the last two centuries, different variants have been considered the _____.
    a. Metric system
    b. 1-center problem
    c. Nonlinear system
    d. George Dantzig

5. The _____ of any solid, plasma, vacuum or theoretical object is how much three-dimensional space it occupies, often quantified numerically. One-dimensional figures and two-dimensional shapes are assigned zero _____ in the three-dimensional space. _____ is presented as ml or cm^3.

    _____s of straight-edged and circular shapes are calculated using arithmetic formulae.

    a. Volume
    b. Cauchy momentum equation
    c. Thermodynamic limit
    d. Stress-energy tensor

6. In geometry and trigonometry, an _____ is the figure formed by two rays sharing a common endpoint, called the vertex of the _____. The magnitude of the _____ is the 'amount of rotation' that separates the two rays, and can be measured by considering the length of circular arc swept out when one ray is rotated about the vertex to coincide with the other. Where there is no possibility of confusion, the term '_____' is used interchangeably for both the geometric configuration itself and for its angular magnitude.
    a. A posteriori
    b. A chemical equation
    c. A Mathematical Theory of Communication
    d. Angle

7. A _____ is a software program that facilitates symbolic mathematics. The core functionality of a CAS is manipulation of mathematical expressions in symbolic form.

The symbolic manipulations supported typically include

- simplification to the smallest possible expression or some standard form, including automatic simplification with assumptions and simplification with constraints
- substitution of symbolic, functors or numeric values for expressions
- change of form of expressions: expanding products and powers, partial and full factorization, rewriting as partial fractions, constraint satisfaction, rewriting trigonometric functions as exponentials, etc.
- partial and total differentiation
- symbolic constrained and unconstrained global optimization
- solution of linear and some non-linear equations over various domains
- solution of some differential and difference equations
- taking some limits
- some indefinite and definite integration, including multidimensional integrals
- integral transforms
- arbitrary-precision numeric operations
- Series operations such as expansion, summation and products
- matrix operations including products, inverses, etc.
- display of mathematical expressions in two-dimensional mathematical form, often using typesetting systems similar to TeX
- add-ons for use in applied mathematics such as physics packages for physical computation
- plotting graphs and parametric plots of functions in two and three dimensions, and animating them
- APIs for linking it on an external program such as a database, or using in a programming language to use the _____
- drawing charts and diagrams
- string manipulation such as matching and searching
- statistical computation
- Theorem proving and verification
- graphic production and editing such as CGI and signal processing as image processing
- sound synthesis

Many also include a programming language, allowing users to implement their own algorithms.

Some _____s focus on a specific area of application; these are typically developed in academia and are free.

a. Computer algebra system
b. 2-3 heap
c. 1-center problem
d. 120-cell

Chapter 7. Measurement and Proportion

8. In mathematics, a _____ is a picture of a straight line in which the integers are shown as specially-marked points evenly spaced on the line. Although this image only shows the integers from -9 to 9, the line includes all real numbers, continuing 'forever' in each direction. It is often used as an aid in teaching simple addition and subtraction, especially involving negative numbers.
   a. Point plotting
   b. Real number
   c. Number system
   d. Number line

9. In geometry, a _____ is defined as a quadrilateral where all four of its angles are right angles.
   a. Polytope
   b. Cantor-Dedekind axiom
   c. Rectangle
   d. Point group in two dimensions

10. In the physical sciences, _____ is a measurement of the gravitational force acting on an object. Near the surface of the Earth, the acceleration due to gravity is approximately constant; this means that an object's _____ is roughly proportional to its mass.

In commerce and in many other applications, _____ means the same as mass as that term is used in physics.

   a. Weight
   b. 120-cell
   c. 2-3 heap
   d. 1-center problem

11. In mathematics, an _____ in the sense of ring theory is a subring $\mathcal{O}$ of a ring R that satisfies the conditions

   1. R is a ring which is a finite-dimensional algebra over the rational number field $\mathbb{Q}$
   2. $\mathcal{O}$ spans R over $\mathbb{Q}$, so that $\mathbb{Q}\mathcal{O} = R$, and
   3. $\mathcal{O}$ is a lattice in R.

The third condition can be stated more accurately, in terms of the extension of scalars of R to the real numbers, embedding R in a real vector space. In less formal terms, additively $\mathcal{O}$ should be a free abelian group generated by a basis for R over $\mathbb{Q}$.

The leading example is the case where R is a number field K and $\mathcal{O}$ is its ring of integers. In algebraic number theory there are examples for any K other than the rational field of proper subrings of the ring of integers that are also _____s.

a. Order
b. Algebraic
c. Efficiency
d. Annihilator

12. In algebra and computer programming, when a number or expression is both preceded and followed by a binary operation, a rule is required for which operation should be applied first; this rule is known as an _____ . From the earliest use of mathematical notation, multiplication took precedence over addition, whichever side of a number it appeared on. Thus 3 + 4 × 5 = 5 × 4 + 3 = 23.
    a. Isomorphism class
    b. Identity element
    c. Order of Operations
    d. Algebraic K-theory

13. _____ is a quantity expressing the two-dimensional size of a defined part of a surface, typically a region bounded by a closed curve. The term surface _____ refers to the total _____ of the exposed surface of a 3-dimensional solid, such as the sum of the _____s of the exposed sides of a polyhedron. _____ is an important invariant in the differential geometry of surfaces.
    a. A posteriori
    b. Area
    c. A Mathematical Theory of Communication
    d. A chemical equation

14. _____ is a conceptual tool often applied in physics, chemistry, engineering, mathematics and statistics to understand physical situations involving a mix of different kinds of physical quantities. It is routinely used by physical scientists and engineers to check the plausibility of derived equations and computations. It is also used to form reasonable hypotheses about complex physical situations that can be tested by experiment or by more developed theories of the phenomena.
    a. 120-cell
    b. 2-3 heap
    c. 1-center problem
    d. Dimensional analysis

15. In mathematics, specifically in topology, a _____ is a two-dimensional manifold. The most familiar examples are those that arise as the boundaries of solid objects in ordinary three-dimensional Euclidean space, EÂ³. On the other hand, there are also more exotic _____s, that are so 'contorted' that they cannot be embedded in three-dimensional space at all.

Chapter 7. Measurement and Proportion

a. Homoeoid
b. Surface
c. Standard torus
d. Cross-cap

16. _____ is how much exposed area an object has. It is expressed in square units. If an object has flat faces, its _____ can be calculated by adding together the areas of its faces.
    a. Compactness measure of a shape
    b. Surface area
    c. Reflection group
    d. Relative dimension

17. In statistics, _____ has two related meanings:

    - the arithmetic _____.
    - the expected value of a random variable, which is also called the population _____.

It is sometimes stated that the '_____' _____s average. This is incorrect if '_____' is taken in the specific sense of 'arithmetic _____' as there are different types of averages: the _____, median, and mode. For instance, average house prices almost always use the median value for the average.

For a real-valued random variable X, the _____ is the expectation of X.

   a. Probability
   b. Statistical population
   c. Proportional hazards model
   d. Mean

18. _____ is a special mathematical relationship between two quantities. Two quantities are called proportional if they vary in such a way that one of the quantities is a constant multiple of the other, or equivalently if they have a constant ratio.
    a. Depth
    b. Compression
    c. Discontinuity
    d. Proportionality

19. In mathematics, a _____ is a constant multiplicative factor of a certain object. For example, in the expression $9x^2$, the _____ of x^2 is 9.

The object can be such things as a variable, a vector, a function, etc.

a. Coefficient
b. Stability radius
c. Fibonacci polynomials
d. Multivariate division algorithm

20. In mathematics, the _____ of a number n is the number that, when added to n, yields zero. The _____ of n is denoted −n. For example, 7 is −7, because 7 + (−7) = 0, and the _____ of −0.3 is 0.3, because −0.3 + 0.3 = 0.

a. Associativity
b. Algebraic structure
c. Arity
d. Additive inverse

21. In mathematics, a _____ is an algebraic structure consisting of a set together with an operation that combines any two of its elements to form a third element. To qualify as a _____, the set and operation must satisfy a few conditions called _____ axioms, namely associativity, identity and invertibility. While these are familiar from many mathematical structures, such as number systems--for example, the integers endowed with the addition operation form a _____--the formulation of the axioms is detached from the concrete nature of the _____ and its operation.

a. Characteristic function
b. Coherence
c. Derivative algebra
d. Group

22. In mathematics, an _____, or central tendency of a data set refers to a measure of the 'middle' or 'expected' value of the data set. There are many different descriptive statistics that can be chosen as a measurement of the central tendency of the data items.

An _____ is a single value that is meant to typify a list of values.

a. A Mathematical Theory of Communication
b. A posteriori
c. A chemical equation
d. Average

Chapter 8. Percent

1. Exponentiation is a mathematical operation, written a^n, involving two numbers, the base a and the _____ n. When n is a positive integer, exponentiation corresponds to repeated multiplication:

$$a^n = \underbrace{a \times \cdots \times a}_{n},$$

just as multiplication by a positive integer corresponds to repeated addition:

$$a \times n = \underbrace{a + \cdots + a}_{n}.$$

The _____ is usually shown as a superscript to the right of the base. The exponentiation a^n can be read as: a raised to the n-th power, a raised to the power [of] n or possibly a raised to the _____ [of] n, or more briefly: a to the n-th power or a to the power [of] n, or even more briefly: a to the n.

   a. Exponential tree
   b. Exponent
   c. Exponential sum
   d. Exponentiating by squaring

2. A _____ is one of the basic shapes of geometry: a polygon with three corners or vertices and three sides or edges which are line segments. A _____ with vertices A, B, and C is denoted ABC.

In Euclidean geometry any three non-collinear points determine a unique _____ and a unique plane.

   a. 1-center problem
   b. Kepler triangle
   c. Fuhrmann circle
   d. Triangle

3. In mathematics, an _____ in the sense of ring theory is a subring $\mathcal{O}$ of a ring R that satisfies the conditions

   1. R is a ring which is a finite-dimensional algebra over the rational number field $\mathbb{Q}$
   2. $\mathcal{O}$ spans R over $\mathbb{Q}$, so that $\mathbb{Q}\mathcal{O} = R$, and
   3. $\mathcal{O}$ is a lattice in R.

The third condition can be stated more accurately, in terms of the extension of scalars of R to the real numbers, embedding R in a real vector space. In less formal terms, additively $\mathcal{O}$ should be a free abelian group generated by a basis for R over $\mathbb{Q}$.

The leading example is the case where R is a number field K and 𝒪 is its ring of integers. In algebraic number theory there are examples for any K other than the rational field of proper subrings of the ring of integers that are also _____s.

   a. Efficiency
   b. Algebraic
   c. Order
   d. Annihilator

4. In algebra and computer programming, when a number or expression is both preceded and followed by a binary operation, a rule is required for which operation should be applied first; this rule is known as an _____ . From the earliest use of mathematical notation, multiplication took precedence over addition, whichever side of a number it appeared on. Thus $3 + 4 \times 5 = 5 \times 4 + 3 = 23$.
   a. Identity element
   b. Order of Operations
   c. Isomorphism class
   d. Algebraic K-theory

5. In mathematics and computer science, _____ (also base-16, hexa or base, of 16. It uses sixteen distinct symbols, most often the symbols 0-9 to represent values zero to nine, and A, B, C, D, E, F (or a through f) to represent values ten to fifteen.

Its primary use is as a human friendly representation of binary coded values, so it is often used in digital electronics and computer engineering.

   a. Radix
   b. Tetradecimal
   c. Factoradic
   d. Hexadecimal

6. _____ is the mathematical operation of scaling one number by another. It is one of the four basic operations in elementary arithmetic.

_____ is defined for whole numbers in terms of repeated addition; for example, 4 multiplied by 3 can be calculated by adding 3 copies of 4 together:

$$4 + 4 + 4 = 12.$$

_____ of rational numbers and real numbers is defined by systematic generalization of this basic idea.

a. Least common multiple
b. The number 0 is even.
c. Highest common factor
d. Multiplication

7. A _____ is a deliberate process for transforming one or more inputs into one or more results, with variable change.

The term is used in a variety of senses, from the very definite arithmetical using an algorithm to the vague heuristics of calculating a strategy in a competition or calculating the chance of a successful relationship between two people.

Multiplying 7 by 8 is a simple algorithmic _____.

a. Mathematical maturity
b. Mathematics Subject Classification
c. Mathematical object
d. Calculation

8. A _____ is a three-dimensional geometric shape that tapers smoothly from a flat, round base to a point called the apex or vertex. More precisely, it is the solid figure bounded by a plane base and the surface formed by the locus of all straight line segments joining the apex to the perimeter of the base. The term '_____' sometimes refers just to the surface of this solid figure, or just to the lateral surface.
a. Blocking
b. Characteristic
c. Gravity waves
d. Cone

9. _____ is a special mathematical relationship between two quantities. Two quantities are called proportional if they vary in such a way that one of the quantities is a constant multiple of the other, or equivalently if they have a constant ratio.
a. Compression
b. Depth
c. Discontinuity
d. Proportionality

10. A _____ is a software program that facilitates symbolic mathematics. The core functionality of a CAS is manipulation of mathematical expressions in symbolic form.

The symbolic manipulations supported typically include

- simplification to the smallest possible expression or some standard form, including automatic simplification with assumptions and simplification with constraints
- substitution of symbolic, functors or numeric values for expressions
- change of form of expressions: expanding products and powers, partial and full factorization, rewriting as partial fractions, constraint satisfaction, rewriting trigonometric functions as exponentials, etc.
- partial and total differentiation
- symbolic constrained and unconstrained global optimization
- solution of linear and some non-linear equations over various domains
- solution of some differential and difference equations
- taking some limits
- some indefinite and definite integration, including multidimensional integrals
- integral transforms
- arbitrary-precision numeric operations
- Series operations such as expansion, summation and products
- matrix operations including products, inverses, etc.
- display of mathematical expressions in two-dimensional mathematical form, often using typesetting systems similar to TeX
- add-ons for use in applied mathematics such as physics packages for physical computation
- plotting graphs and parametric plots of functions in two and three dimensions, and animating them
- APIs for linking it on an external program such as a database, or using in a programming language to use the _____
- drawing charts and diagrams
- string manipulation such as matching and searching
- statistical computation
- Theorem proving and verification
- graphic production and editing such as CGI and signal processing as image processing
- sound synthesis

Many also include a programming language, allowing users to implement their own algorithms.

Some _____s focus on a specific area of application; these are typically developed in academia and are free.

a. 2-3 heap
b. 120-cell
c. Computer algebra system
d. 1-center problem

11. In economics, business, retail, and accounting, a _____ is the value of money that has been used up to produce something, and hence is not available for use anymore. In business, the _____ may be one of acquisition, in which case the amount of money expended to acquire it is counted as _____. In this case, money is the input that is gone in order to acquire the thing.

   a. 120-cell
   b. 1-center problem
   c. 2-3 heap
   d. Cost

12. _____ is a lightweight markup language, originally created by John Gruber and Aaron Swartz to help maximum readability and 'publishability' of both its input and output forms. The language takes many cues from existing conventions for marking up plain text in email. _____ converts its marked-up text input to valid, well-formed XHTML and replaces left-pointing angle brackets ('<') and ampersands with their corresponding character entity references.

   a. 2-3 heap
   b. 120-cell
   c. 1-center problem
   d. Markdown

13. _____ is a fee, paid on borrowed capital. Assets lent include money, shares, consumer goods through hire purchase, major assets such as aircraft, and even entire factories in finance lease arrangements. The _____ is calculated upon the value of the assets in the same manner as upon money.

   a. Interest sensitivity gap
   b. A Mathematical Theory of Communication
   c. Interest
   d. Interest expense

14. In abstract algebra, a module S over a ring R is called _____ or irreducible if it is not the zero module 0 and if its only submodules are 0 and S. Understanding the _____ modules over a ring is usually helpful because these modules form the 'building blocks' of all other modules in a certain sense.

Abelian groups are the same as Z-modules.

   a. Harmonic series
   b. Basis
   c. Derivation
   d. Simple

15. In mathematics, a _____ is an algebraic structure consisting of a set together with an operation that combines any two of its elements to form a third element. To qualify as a _____, the set and operation must satisfy a few conditions called _____ axioms, namely associativity, identity and invertibility. While these are familiar from many mathematical structures, such as number systems--for example, the integers endowed with the addition operation form a _____--the formulation of the axioms is detached from the concrete nature of the _____ and its operation.
   a. Coherence
   b. Derivative algebra
   c. Characteristic function
   d. Group

16. _____ is the statistical study of all populations. It can be a very general science that can be applied to any kind of dynamic population, that is, one that changes over time or space. It encompasses the study of the size, structure and distribution of populations, and spatial and/or temporal changes in them in response to birth, migration, aging and death.
   a. 1-center problem
   b. 120-cell
   c. 2-3 heap
   d. Demography

Chapter 9. Geometry

1. Exponentiation is a mathematical operation, written a^n, involving two numbers, the base a and the _____ n. When n is a positive integer, exponentiation corresponds to repeated multiplication:

$$a^n = \underbrace{a \times \cdots \times a}_{n},$$

just as multiplication by a positive integer corresponds to repeated addition:

$$a \times n = \underbrace{a + \cdots + a}_{n}.$$

The _____ is usually shown as a superscript to the right of the base. The exponentiation a^n can be read as: a raised to the n-th power, a raised to the power [of] n or possibly a raised to the _____ [of] n, or more briefly: a to the n-th power or a to the power [of] n, or even more briefly: a to the n.

   a. Exponential sum
   b. Exponent
   c. Exponentiating by squaring
   d. Exponential tree

2. A _____ is one of the basic shapes of geometry: a polygon with three corners or vertices and three sides or edges which are line segments. A _____ with vertices A, B, and C is denoted ABC.

In Euclidean geometry any three non-collinear points determine a unique _____ and a unique plane.

   a. Fuhrmann circle
   b. Kepler triangle
   c. 1-center problem
   d. Triangle

3. _____ is a part of mathematics concerned with questions of size, shape, and relative position of figures and with properties of space. _____ is one of the oldest sciences. Initially a body of practical knowledge concerning lengths, areas, and volumes, in the third century BC _____ was put into an axiomatic form by Euclid, whose treatment--Euclidean _____ --set a standard for many centuries to follow.

   a. 1-center problem
   b. 2-3 heap
   c. Geometry
   d. 120-cell

4. In geometry, a _____ is a part of a line that is bounded by two distinct end points, and contains every point on the line between its end points. Examples of _____s include the sides of a triangle or square. More generally, when the end points are both vertices of a polygon, the _____ is either an edge if they are adjacent vertices, or otherwise a diagonal.
   a. Transversal line
   b. Cuboid
   c. Golden angle
   d. Line segment

5. In mathematics, a _____ is, informally, an infinitely vast and infinitely thin sheet. _____s may be thought of as objects in some higher dimensional space, or they may be considered without any outside space, as in the setting of Euclidean geometry
   a. Blocking
   b. Bandwidth
   c. Group
   d. Plane

6. In mathematics, the _____ is an approach to finding a particular solution to certain inhomogeneous ordinary differential equations and recurrence relations. It is closely related to the annihilator method, but instead of using a particular kind of differential operator in order to find the best possible form of the particular solution, a 'guess' is made as to the appropriate form, which is then tested by differentiating the resulting equation. In this sense, the _____ is less formal but more intuitive than the annihilator method.
   a. Phase line
   b. Differential algebraic equations
   c. Linear differential equation
   d. Method of undetermined coefficients

7. In geometry and trigonometry, an _____ is the figure formed by two rays sharing a common endpoint, called the vertex of the _____. The magnitude of the _____ is the 'amount of rotation' that separates the two rays, and can be measured by considering the length of circular arc swept out when one ray is rotated about the vertex to coincide with the other. Where there is no possibility of confusion, the term '_____' is used interchangeably for both the geometric configuration itself and for its angular magnitude.
   a. A chemical equation
   b. A posteriori
   c. A Mathematical Theory of Communication
   d. Angle

Chapter 9. Geometry

8. In mathematics the concept of a _____ generalizes notions such as 'length', 'area', and 'volume'. Informally, given some base set, a '_____' is any consistent assignment of 'sizes' to the subsets of the base set. Depending on the application, the 'size' of a subset may be interpreted as its physical size, the amount of something that lies within the subset, or the probability that some random process will yield a result within the subset.
    a. Congruent
    b. Cusp
    c. Lattice
    d. Measure

9. A _____ of a curve is the envelope of a family of congruent circles centered on the curve. It generalises the concept of _____ lines.

It is sometimes called the offset curve but the term 'offset' often refers also to translation.

    a. Cycloid
    b. Parallel
    c. Bifolium
    d. Cissoid

10. The existence and properties of _____ are the basis of Euclid's parallel postulate. _____ are two lines on the same plane that do not intersect even assuming that lines extend to infinity in either direction.
    a. Parallel lines
    b. Spidron
    c. Vertical translation
    d. Square wheel

11. In geometry, a _____ is a special kind of point, usually a corner of a polygon, polyhedron, or higher dimensional polytope. In the geometry of curves a _____ is a point of where the first derivative of curvature is zero. In graph theory, a _____ is the fundamental unit out of which graphs are formed
    a. Crib
    b. Dini
    c. Duality
    d. Vertex

12. In mathematics, the _____ of a real number is its numerical value without regard to its sign. So, for example, 3 is the _____ of both 3 and −3.

The _____ of a number a is denoted by $|a|$.

Generalizations of the _____ for real numbers occur in a wide variety of mathematical settings.

a. Absolute value
b. Area hyperbolic functions
c. A chemical equation
d. A Mathematical Theory of Communication

13. A pair of angles are complementary if the sum of their measures add up to 90 degrees.

If the two _____ are adjacent (i.e. have a common vertex and share a side, but do not have any interior points in common) their non-shared sides form a right angle.

In Euclidean geometry, the two acute angles in a right triangle are complementary, because there are 180>° in a triangle and 90>° have been accounted for by the right angle.

a. Conway polyhedron notation
b. Hypotenuse
c. Quincunx
d. Complementary angles

14. In geometry and trigonometry, a _____ is defined as an angle between two straight intersecting lines of ninety degrees, or one-quarter of a circle.
a. Trigonometric functions
b. Sine integral
c. Trigonometry
d. Right angle

15. An angle smaller than a right angle is called an _____ (less than 90 degrees).
a. Ultraparallel theorem
b. Euclidean geometry
c. Acute angle
d. Integral geometry

16. _____ is an adjective meaning contiguous, adjoining or abutting.

In geometry, _____ is when sides meet to make an angle.

Chapter 9. Geometry

In trigonometry the _____ side of a right angled triangle is the cathetus next to the angle in question.

a. Affine geometry
b. Adjacent
c. Ordered geometry
d. Ambient space

17. In geometry, _____ are angles that have a common ray coming out of the vertex going between two other rays. In other words, they are angles that are side by side, or adjacent.

An angle with a ray connected to a common point down the center.

a. Erlangen Program
b. A Mathematical Theory of Communication
c. Adjacent angles
d. Elliptic geometry

18. An angle equal to two right angles is called a _____ (equal to 180 degrees).
a. Straight angle
b. Householder transformation
c. Loomis-Whitney inequality
d. Theorem

19. A pair of angles is _____ if their measurements add up to 180 degrees. If the two _____ angles are adjacent their non-shared sides form a straight line. The supplement of 135 would be 45.
a. Cylinder
b. Supplementary
c. Dense
d. FISH

20. A pair of angles are said to be _____ if they share the same vertex and are bounded by the same pair of lines but are opposite to each other. They are also congruent.

a. Reflection symmetry
b. Hinge theorem
c. Vertical angles
d. Line segment

21. _____ are formed when a given transversal line crosses two coplanar lines. The _____ are not necessarily congruent. In the event that the _____ are congruent, these angles can be used to determine the degrees of the other angles of the parallel lines.
 a. Brocard circle
 b. Prismatic pentagonal tiling
 c. Corresponding angles
 d. Conformal connection

22. In general topology and related areas of mathematics, the _____ (inductive topology or strong topology) on a set X, with respect to a family of functions into X, is the finest topology on X which makes those functions continuous.

Given a set X and a family of topological spaces Y_i with functions

$$f_i : Y_i \to X$$

the _____ τ on X is the finest topology such that each

$$f_i : Y_i \to (X, \tau)$$

is continuous.

Explicitly, the _____ may be described as follows: a subset U of X is open if and only if $f_i^{-1}(U)$ is open in Y_i for each i ∈ I.

 a. Wallman compactification
 b. Cylinder set
 c. Gluing axiom
 d. Final topology

23. An _____ is an angle formed by one side of a simple polygon and a line extended from that side.

a. Exterior angle
b. Interior angle
c. Orthogon
d. Angular diameter

24. In geometry, an _____ is an angle formed by two sides of a simple polygon that share an endpoint, namely, the angle on the inner side of the polygon. A simple polygon has exactly one internal angle per vertex.

If every internal angle of a polygon is at most 180 degrees, the polygon is called convex.

   a. Interior angle
   b. Angle bisector
   c. Angle chasing
   d. Exterior angle

25. In combinatorial mathematics, given a collection C of sets, a _____ is a set containing exactly one element from each member of the collection: it is a section of the quotient map induced by the collection. If the original sets are not disjoint, there are several different definitions. One variation is that there is a bijection f from the _____ to C such that x is an element of f
   a. Combinadic
   b. Transversal
   c. Heawood number
   d. Combinatorial design

26. In geometry, an _____ is a triangle in which all three sides have equal lengths. In traditional or Euclidean geometry, _____s are also equiangular; that is, all three internal angles are also equal to each other and are each 60°. They are regular polygons, and can therefore also be referred to as regular triangles.
   a. A Mathematical Theory of Communication
   b. A chemical equation
   c. Isotomic conjugate
   d. Equilateral triangle

27. In geometry, a _____ is a polygon with seven sides and seven angles. In a regular _____, in which all sides and all angles are equal, the sides meet at an angle of 5π/7 radians, 128.5714286 degrees. Its Schläfli symbol is {7}.

a. Pentagon
b. Heptagon
c. Heptadecagon
d. Hexagon

28. In geometry, a _____ is a polygon with six edges and six vertices. A regular _____ has Schläfli symbol {6}.

The internal angles of a regular _____ are all 120° and the _____ has 720 degrees.

a. Decagon
b. Polygonal curve
c. Polygonal chain
d. Hexagon

29. In geometry, a _____ (or enneagon) is a nine-sided polygon.

The name '_____' is a hybrid formation, from Latin (nonus, 'ninth' + gonon), used equivalently, attested already in the 16th century in French nonogone and in English from the 17th century. The name 'enneagon' comes from Greek enneagonon, (εννεα, nine + γωνον (from γωνῖα = corner)), and is arguably more correct, though somewhat less common.

a. Parallelogon
b. Regular decagon
c. Dodecagon
d. Nonagon

30. In geometry, an _____ is a polygon that has eight sides. A regular _____ is represented by the Schläfli symbol {8}. A regular _____ is constructible with compass and straightedge.

a. Equilateral polygon
b. A Mathematical Theory of Communication
c. Enneagon
d. Octagon

31. In geometry, a _____ is any five-sided polygon. A _____ may be simple or self-intersecting. The internal angles in a simple _____ total 540°.

a. Triskaidecagon
b. Pentagon
c. Star polygon
d. Regular octagon

32. In geometry a _____ is traditionally a plane figure that is bounded by a closed path or circuit, composed of a finite sequence of straight line segments. These segments are called its edges or sides, and the points where two edges meet are the _____'s vertices or corners. The interior of the _____ is sometimes called its body.
a. Polygonal curve
b. Parallelogon
c. Regular polygon
d. Polygon

33. In mathematics, the _____ or Pythagoras' theorem is a relation in Euclidean geometry among the three sides of a right triangle. The theorem is named after the Greek mathematician Pythagoras, who by tradition is credited with its discovery and proof, although it is often argued that knowledge of the theory predates him.. The theorem is as follows:

In any right triangle, the area of the square whose side is the hypotenuse is equal to the sum of the areas of the squares whose sides are the two legs.

a. 120-cell
b. 2-3 heap
c. 1-center problem
d. Pythagorean Theorem

34. In geometry, a _____ is a polygon with four sides or edges and four vertices or corners. Sometimes, the term quadrangle is used, for etymological symmetry with triangle, and sometimes tetragon for consistency with pentagon, hexagon and so on. The interior angles of a _____ add up to 360 degrees of arc.
a. 1-center problem
b. 2-3 heap
c. 120-cell
d. Quadrilateral

35. A _____ is a polygon which is equiangular and equilateral. _____s may be convex or star.

These properties apply to both convex and star _____s.

a. Constructible polygon
b. Star-shaped polygon
c. Regular polygon
d. Regular decagon

36. In mathematics, a _____ is a statement that can be proved on the basis of explicitly stated or previously agreed assumptions.
   a. Logical value
   b. Disjunction introduction
   c. Boolean function
   d. Theorem

37. An _____ is a quadrilateral with a line of symmetry bisecting one pair of opposite sides, making it automatically a trapezoid. Two opposite sides are parallel, the two other sides are of equal length. The diagonals are of equal length.
   a. Isosceles trapezoid
   b. A posteriori
   c. A Mathematical Theory of Communication
   d. A chemical equation

38. An _____ is a triangle that has one internal angle larger than 90°
   a. Isotomic conjugate
   b. A Mathematical Theory of Communication
   c. A chemical equation
   d. Obtuse triangle

39. In geometry, a _____ is a quadrilateral with two sets of parallel sides. The opposite sides of a _____ are of equal length, and the opposite angles of a _____ are congruent. The three-dimensional counterpart of a _____ is a parallelepiped.
   a. 1-center problem
   b. Parallelogram
   c. 2-3 heap
   d. 120-cell

40. The _____ is the length of the line that bounds an area In the special case where the area is circular, the _____ is known as the circumference.

a. Perimeter
b. Multilateration
c. Concyclic
d. Reflection symmetry

41. In geometry, a _____ is defined as a quadrilateral where all four of its angles are right angles.
a. Rectangle
b. Polytope
c. Cantor-Dedekind axiom
d. Point group in two dimensions

42. In geometry, a _____ , or rhomb is an equilateral parallelogram. In other words, it is a four-sided polygon in which every side has the same length.

The _____ is often casually called a diamond, after the diamonds suit in playing cards, or a lozenge, because those shapes are rhombi, although rhombi are not necessarily diamonds or lozenges.

a. 2-3 heap
b. 120-cell
c. 1-center problem
d. Rhombus

43. A _____ or a trapezium is a quadrilateral that has at least one pair of parallel lines for sides.

Some authors define it as a quadrilateral having exactly one pair of parallel sides, so as to exclude parallelograms, which otherwise would be regarded as a special type of _____, but most mathematicians use the inclusive definition.

In North America, the term trapezium is used to refer to a quadrilateral with no parallel sides.

a. Trapezium
b. Rhomboid
c. Lozenge
d. Trapezoid

44. In set theory and its applications throughout mathematics, a _____ is a collection of sets that can be unambiguously defined by a property that all its members share. The precise definition of '_____' depends on foundational context. In work on ZF set theory, the notion of _____ is informal, whereas other set theories, such as NBG set theory, axiomatize the notion of '_____'.

   a. Coherence
   b. Filter
   c. Congruent
   d. Class

45. The term _____ or centre is used in various contexts in abstract algebra to denote the set of all those elements that commute with all other elements. More specifically:

   - The _____ of a group G consists of all those elements x in G such that xg = gx for all g in G. This is a normal subgroup of G.
   - The _____ of a ring R is the subset of R consisting of all those elements x of R such that xr = rx for all r in R. The _____ is a commutative subring of R, so R is an algebra over its _____.
   - The _____ of an algebra A consists of all those elements x of A such that xa = ax for all a in A. See also: central simple algebra.
   - The _____ of a Lie algebra L consists of all those elements x in L such that [x,a] = 0 for all a in L. This is an ideal of the Lie algebra L.
   - The _____ of a monoidal category C consists of pairs *a natural isomorphism satisfying certain axioms*.

   a. Disk
   b. Block size
   c. Brute Force
   d. Center

46. A _____ is a simple shape of Euclidean geometry consisting of those points in a plane which are at a constant distance, called the radius, from a fixed point, called the center. A _____ with center A is sometimes denoted by the symbol A.

   A chord of a _____ is a line segment whose two endpoints lie on the _____.

   a. Malfatti circles
   b. Circular segment
   c. Circle
   d. Circumcircle

47. The _____ is the distance around a closed curve. _____ is a kind of perimeter.

The _____ of a circle is the length around it.

a. Brascamp-Lieb inequality
b. Flatness
c. Compactness measure of a shape
d. Circumference

48. In mathematics, an _____ in the sense of ring theory is a subring $\mathcal{O}$ of a ring R that satisfies the conditions

1. R is a ring which is a finite-dimensional algebra over the rational number field $\mathbb{Q}$
2. $\mathcal{O}$ spans R over $\mathbb{Q}$, so that $\mathbb{Q}\mathcal{O} = R$, and
3. $\mathcal{O}$ is a lattice in R.

The third condition can be stated more accurately, in terms of the extension of scalars of R to the real numbers, embedding R in a real vector space. In less formal terms, additively $\mathcal{O}$ should be a free abelian group generated by a basis for R over $\mathbb{Q}$.

The leading example is the case where R is a number field K and $\mathcal{O}$ is its ring of integers. In algebraic number theory there are examples for any K other than the rational field of proper subrings of the ring of integers that are also _____s.

a. Efficiency
b. Algebraic
c. Annihilator
d. Order

49. In algebra and computer programming, when a number or expression is both preceded and followed by a binary operation, a rule is required for which operation should be applied first; this rule is known as an _____ . From the earliest use of mathematical notation, multiplication took precedence over addition, whichever side of a number it appeared on. Thus 3 + 4 × 5 = 5 × 4 + 3 = 23.
a. Algebraic K-theory
b. Isomorphism class
c. Identity element
d. Order of Operations

50. In classical geometry, a _____ of a circle or sphere is any line segment from its center to its boundary. By extension, the _____ of a circle or sphere is the length of any such segment. The _____ is half the diameter. In science and engineering the term _____ of curvature is commonly used as a synonym for _____.

a. Duoprism
b. Radius
c. Non-Euclidean geometry
d. Birational geometry

51. _____ is a quantity expressing the two-dimensional size of a defined part of a surface, typically a region bounded by a closed curve. The term surface _____ refers to the total _____ of the exposed surface of a 3-dimensional solid, such as the sum of the _____s of the exposed sides of a polyhedron. _____ is an important invariant in the differential geometry of surfaces.
   a. Area
   b. A Mathematical Theory of Communication
   c. A posteriori
   d. A chemical equation

52. A _____ is a number that can be represented as a regular and discrete geometric pattern. If the pattern is polytopic, the figurate is labeled a polytopic number, and may be a polygonal number or a polyhedral number.

The first few triangular numbers can be built from rows of 1, 2, 3, 4, 5, and 6 items:

The n-th regular r-topic number is given by the formula:

$$P_r(n) = \binom{n+r-1}{r} = \frac{n^{(r)}}{r!} \quad \text{for } n \geq 1$$

r! is the factorial of r, $\binom{n}{r}$ is a binomial coefficient, and n is the rising factorial.

   a. Heptagonal number
   b. Square number
   c. Figurate number
   d. Centered pentagonal number

53. In mathematics, a _____, sometimes also called a perfect square, is an integer that can be written as the square of some other integer; in other words, it is the product of some integer with itself. So, for example, 9 is a _____, since it can be written as 3 × 3. _____s are non-negative.

Chapter 9. Geometry

a. Pentagonal pyramidal number
b. Centered pentagonal number
c. Hexagonal number
d. Square number

54. In mathematics and computer science, _____ (also base-16, hexa or base, of 16. It uses sixteen distinct symbols, most often the symbols 0-9 to represent values zero to nine, and A, B, C, D, E, F (or a through f) to represent values ten to fifteen.

Its primary use is as a human friendly representation of binary coded values, so it is often used in digital electronics and computer engineering.

a. Factoradic
b. Hexadecimal
c. Radix
d. Tetradecimal

55. _____ is the measurement of vertical distance, but has two meanings in common use. It can either indicate how 'tall' something is, or how 'high up' it is. For example one could say 'That is a tall building', or 'That airplane is high up in the sky'.
a. 2-3 heap
b. 1-center problem
c. Height
d. 120-cell

56. A _____ is a three-dimensional geometric shape that tapers smoothly from a flat, round base to a point called the apex or vertex. More precisely, it is the solid figure bounded by a plane base and the surface formed by the locus of all straight line segments joining the apex to the perimeter of the base. The term '_____' sometimes refers just to the surface of this solid figure, or just to the lateral surface.
a. Blocking
b. Characteristic
c. Cone
d. Gravity waves

57. A _____ is the longest side of a right triangle, the side opposite of the right angle. The length of the _____ of a right triangle can be found using the Pythagorean theorem, which states that the square of the length of the _____ equals the sum of the squares of the lengths of the two other sides.

For example, if one of the other sides has a length of 3 meters and the other has a length of 4 m.

  a. Concyclic points
  b. Reflection symmetry
  c. Golden angle
  d. Hypotenuse

58. In a right triangle, the cathetusoriginally from the Greek word Kι¬θετος, plural catheti

- 1 Generally
- 2 References
- 3 See also
- 4 External links

In a wider sense, a _____ is any line falling perpendicularly on another line or a surface. Such a line is more commonly known as a surface normal.

  a. Line segment
  b. Face diagonal
  c. Central angle
  d. Cathetus

59. In mathematics, the _____ of a number n is the number that, when added to n, yields zero. The _____ of n is denoted −n. For example, 7 is −7, because 7 + (−7) = 0, and the _____ of −0.3 is 0.3, because −0.3 + 0.3 = 0.
  a. Arity
  b. Associativity
  c. Algebraic structure
  d. Additive inverse

60. In vascular plants, the _____ is the organ of a plant body that typically lies below the surface of the soil. This is not always the case, however, since a _____ can also be aerial (that is, growing above the ground) or aerating (that is, growing up above the ground or especially above water.) Furthermore, a stem normally occurring below ground is not exceptional either

a. 2-3 heap
b. Root
c. 1-center problem
d. 120-cell

61. In mathematics, a _____ of a number x is a number r such that r² = x, or, in other words, a number r whose square is x. Every non-negative real number x has a unique non-negative _____, called the principal _____, which is denoted with a radical symbol as $\sqrt{x}$, or, using exponent notation, as x^(1/2). For example, the principal _____ of 9 is 3, denoted $\sqrt{9}$ = 3, because 3² = 3 × 3 = 9.
a. Hyperbolic functions
b. Multiplicative inverse
c. Double exponential
d. Square Root

62. In linear algebra, two n-by-n matrices A and B over the field K are called _____ if there exists an invertible n-by-n matrix P over K such that

$$P^{-1}AP = B.$$

One of the meanings of the term similarity transformation is such a transformation of a matrix A into a matrix B.

Similarity is an equivalence relation on the space of square matrices.

_____ matrices share many properties:

- rank
- determinant
- trace
- eigenvalues
- characteristic polynomial
- minimal polynomial
- elementary divisors

There are two reasons for these facts:

- two _____ matrices can be thought of as describing the same linear map, but with respect to different bases
- the map X ↦ P⁻¹XP is an automorphism of the associative algebra of all n-by-n matrices, as the one-object case of the above category of all matrices.

Because of this, for a given matrix A, one is interested in finding a simple 'normal form' B which is _____ to A -- the study of A then reduces to the study of the simpler matrix B.

   a. Dense
   b. Similar
   c. Coherence
   d. Blinding

63.   In category theory, an abstract branch of mathematics, an _____ of a category C is an object I in C such that for every object X in C, there exists precisely one morphism I → X. The dual notion is that of a terminal object: T is terminal if for every object X in C there exists a single morphism X → T. _____s are also called coterminal, and terminal objects are also called final.
   a. A chemical equation
   b. A posteriori
   c. A Mathematical Theory of Communication
   d. Initial object

64.   In geometry, two sets of points are called _____ if one can be transformed into the other by an isometry. Less formally, two figures are _____ if they have the same shape and size, but are in different positions.

In a Euclidean system, congruence is fundamental; it is the counterpart of equality for numbers.

   a. Gamma test
   b. Congruent
   c. Function
   d. Germ

65. _____ is an integrated system of software products provided by _____ Institute that enables the programmer to perform:

- data entry, retrieval, management, and mining
- report writing and graphics
- statistical analysis
- business planning, forecasting, and decision support
- operations research and project management
- quality improvement
- applications development
- data warehousing
- platform independent and remote computing

In addition, _____ has many business solutions that enable large scale software solutions for areas such as IT management, human resource management, financial management, business intelligence, customer relationship management and more.

_____ is driven by _____ programs that define a sequence of operations to be performed on data stored as tables. Although non-programmer graphical user interfaces to _____ exist, most of the time these GUIs are just a front-end to automate or facilitate generation of _____ programs. _____ components expose their functionalities via application programming interfaces, in the form of statements and procedures.

   a. SAS
   b. FISH
   c. Blocking
   d. Conchoid

66. In mathematics, the _____s are analogs of the ordinary trigonometric functions. The basic _____s are the hyperbolic sine 'sinh', and the hyperbolic cosine 'cosh', from which are derived the hyperbolic tangent 'tanh', etc., in analogy to the derived trigonometric functions. The inverse _____ are the area hyperbolic sine 'arsinh' (also called 'asinh', or sometimes by the misnomer of 'arcsinh') and so on.
   a. Heaviside step function
   b. Square root
   c. Rectangular function
   d. Hyperbolic function

67. In common usage, a cylinder is taken to mean a finite section of a right _____ with its ends closed to form two circular surfaces, as in the figure (right.) If the cylinder has a radius r and length (height) h, then its volume is given by

$$V = \pi r^2 h$$

and its surface area is:

- the area of the top (πr^2) +
- the area of the bottom (πr^2) +
- the area of the side $(2\pi r h)$.

Therefore without the top or bottom (lateral area), the surface area is

$$A = 2\pi r h.$$

With the top and bottom, the surface area is

$$A = 2\pi r^2 + 2\pi r h = 2\pi r(r + h).$$

For a given volume, the cylinder with the smallest surface area has h = 2r. For a given surface area, the cylinder with the largest volume has h = 2r, i.e. the cylinder fits in a cube (height = diameter.)

Cylindric sections are the intersections of cylinders with planes.

    a. Circular cylinder
    b. 1-center problem
    c. 2-3 heap
    d. 120-cell

    68. In mathematics, a _____ is a quadric surface, with the following equation in Cartesian coordinates: $(x/a)^2 + (y/b)^2 = 1$.
    a. Derivative algebra
    b. Cylinder
    c. Free
    d. Discontinuity

    69. The term _____ refers to the central sense organ complex, for those animals that have one, normally on the ventral surface of the head and can depending on the definition in the human case, include the hair, forehead, eyebrow, eyes, nose, ears, cheeks, mouth, lips, philtrum, teeth, skin, and chin. The _____ has uses of expression, appearance, and identity amongst others.It also has different senses like smelling, tasting, hearing, and seeing.

Caricatures often exaggerate facial features to make a _____ more easily recognized in association with a pronounced portion of the _____ of the individual in question--for example, a caricature of Osama bin Laden might focus on his facial hair and nose; a caricature of George W. Bush might enlarge his ears to the size of an elephant¢s; a caricature of Jay Leno may pronounce his head and chin; and a caricature of Mick Jagger might enlarge his lips.

  a. Face
  b. 2-3 heap
  c. 1-center problem
  d. 120-cell

70. A _____ is a building where the upper surfaces are triangular and converge on one point. The base of _____s are usually quadrilateral or trilateral, meaning that a _____ usually has four or five faces. A _____'s design, with the majority of the weight closer to the ground, means that less material higher up on the _____ will be pushing down from above.
  a. 120-cell
  b. 2-3 heap
  c. 1-center problem
  d. Pyramid

71. _____ is a three-dimensional geometric shape formed by straight lines through a fixed point vertex to the points of a fixed curve directrix.
  a. Right circular cone
  b. 120-cell
  c. 1-center problem
  d. 2-3 heap

72. In common usage, a cylinder is taken to mean a finite section of a _____ with its ends closed to form two circular surfaces, as in the figure (right.) If the cylinder has a radius r and length (height) h, then its volume is given by

$$V = \pi r^2 h$$

and its surface area is:

- the area of the top (πr^2) +
- the area of the bottom (πr^2) +
- the area of the side $(2\pi r h)$.

Therefore without the top or bottom (lateral area), the surface area is

$$A = 2\pi r h.$$

With the top and bottom, the surface area is

$$A = 2\pi r^2 + 2\pi r h = 2\pi r(r + h).$$

For a given volume, the cylinder with the smallest surface area has h = 2r. For a given surface area, the cylinder with the largest volume has h = 2r, i.e. the cylinder fits in a cube (height = diameter.)

Cylindric sections are the intersections of cylinders with planes.

a. 1-center problem
b. Right circular cylinder
c. 2-3 heap
d. 120-cell

73. A _____ is a symmetrical geometrical object. In non-mathematical usage, the term is used to refer either to a round ball or to its two-dimensional surface. In mathematics, a _____ is the set of all points in three-dimensional space which are at distance r from a fixed point of that space, where r is a positive real number called the radius of the _____.
   a. Lie derivative
   b. Sphere
   c. Differentiable manifold
   d. Differential geometry of curves

74. The _____ of any solid, plasma, vacuum or theoretical object is how much three-dimensional space it occupies, often quantified numerically. One-dimensional figures and two-dimensional shapes are assigned zero _____ in the three-dimensional space. _____ is presented as ml or cm^3.

_____s of straight-edged and circular shapes are calculated using arithmetic formulae.

a. Volume
b. Stress-energy tensor
c. Cauchy momentum equation
d. Thermodynamic limit

75. In mathematics, specifically in topology, a _____ is a two-dimensional manifold. The most familiar examples are those that arise as the boundaries of solid objects in ordinary three-dimensional Euclidean space, EÂ³. On the other hand, there are also more exotic _____s, that are so 'contorted' that they cannot be embedded in three-dimensional space at all.
   a. Cross-cap
   b. Surface
   c. Standard torus
   d. Homoeoid

76. _____ is how much exposed area an object has. It is expressed in square units. If an object has flat faces, its _____ can be calculated by adding together the areas of its faces.
   a. Relative dimension
   b. Reflection group
   c. Compactness measure of a shape
   d. Surface area

77. A _____ number is a positive integer which has a positive divisor other than one or itself. By definition, every integer greater than one is either a prime number or a _____ number.zero and one are considered to be neither prime nor _____. For example, the integer 14 is a _____ number because it can be factored as 2 × 7.
   a. Discontinuity
   b. Key server
   c. Basis
   d. Composite

78. In graph theory, a _____ is a graph whose vertices can be associated with chords of a circle such that two vertices are adjacent if and only if the corresponding chords in the circle intersect.

Spinrad (1994) gives an $O(n^2)$-time recognition algorithm for _____s that also computes a circle model of the input graph if it is a _____.

A number of other problems that are NP-complete on general graphs have polynomial time algorithms when restricted to _____s.

a. Planar graph
b. Vertex-transitive graph
c. Sparse graph
d. Circle graph

79. In mathematics, a _____ is an algebraic structure consisting of a set together with an operation that combines any two of its elements to form a third element. To qualify as a _____, the set and operation must satisfy a few conditions called _____ axioms, namely associativity, identity and invertibility. While these are familiar from many mathematical structures, such as number systems--for example, the integers endowed with the addition operation form a _____--the formulation of the axioms is detached from the concrete nature of the _____ and its operation.
    a. Coherence
    b. Group
    c. Derivative algebra
    d. Characteristic function

80. _____ generally conveys two primary meanings. The first is an imprecise sense of harmonious or aesthetically-pleasing proportionality and balance; such that it reflects beauty or perfection. The second meaning is a precise and well-defined concept of balance or 'patterned self-similarity' that can be demonstrated or proved according to the rules of a formal system: by geometry, through physics or otherwise.
    a. Symmetry breaking
    b. Symmetry
    c. Molecular symmetry
    d. Tessellation

81. A bar chart or _____ is a chart with rectangular bars with lengths proportional to the values that they represent. Bar charts are used for comparing two or more values. The bars can be horizontally or vertically oriented.
    a. Bar graph
    b. 120-cell
    c. 2-3 heap
    d. 1-center problem

Chapter 10. Statistics and Probability

1. Exponentiation is a mathematical operation, written a^n, involving two numbers, the base a and the _____ n. When n is a positive integer, exponentiation corresponds to repeated multiplication:

$$a^n = \underbrace{a \times \cdots \times a}_{n},$$

just as multiplication by a positive integer corresponds to repeated addition:

$$a \times n = \underbrace{a + \cdots + a}_{n}.$$

The _____ is usually shown as a superscript to the right of the base. The exponentiation a^n can be read as: a raised to the n-th power, a raised to the power [of] n or possibly a raised to the _____ [of] n, or more briefly: a to the n-th power or a to the power [of] n, or even more briefly: a to the n.

a. Exponential tree
b. Exponentiating by squaring
c. Exponential sum
d. Exponent

2. A _____ is one of the basic shapes of geometry: a polygon with three corners or vertices and three sides or edges which are line segments. A _____ with vertices A, B, and C is denoted ABC.

In Euclidean geometry any three non-collinear points determine a unique _____ and a unique plane.

a. Fuhrmann circle
b. Triangle
c. 1-center problem
d. Kepler triangle

3. In set theory and its applications throughout mathematics, a _____ is a collection of sets that can be unambiguously defined by a property that all its members share. The precise definition of '_____' depends on foundational context. In work on ZF set theory, the notion of _____ is informal, whereas other set theories, such as NBG set theory, axiomatize the notion of '_____'.

a. Congruent
b. Filter
c. Class
d. Coherence

4. In differential geometry, a discipline within mathematics, a _____ is a subset of the tangent bundle of a manifold satisfying certain properties. _____s are used to build up notions of integrability, and specifically of a foliation of a manifold
   a. Discontinuity
   b. Distribution
   c. Constraint
   d. Coherence

5. In statistics the _____ of an event i is the number n_i of times the event occurred in the experiment or the study. These frequencies are often graphically represented in histograms.

We speak of absolute frequencies, when the counts n_i themselves are given and of

$$f_i = \frac{n_i}{N} = \frac{n_i}{\sum_i n_i}$$

Taking the f_i for all i and tabulating or plotting them leads to a _____ distribution.

   a. Robinson-Dadson curves
   b. Subharmonic
   c. Digital room correction
   d. Frequency

6. In statistics, a _____ is a list of the values that a variable takes in a sample. It is usually a list, ordered by quantity, showing the number of times each value appears. For example, if 100 people rate a five-point Likert scale assessing their agreement with a statement on a scale on which 1 denotes strong agreement and 5 strong disagreement, the _____ of their responses might look like:

This simple tabulation has two drawbacks.

   a. Frequency distribution
   b. Confounding
   c. Percentile
   d. Covariance

7. In descriptive statistics, the _____ is the length of the smallest interval which contains all the data. It is calculated by subtracting the smallest observations from the greatest and provides an indication of statistical dispersion.

It is measured in the same units as the data.

Chapter 10. Statistics and Probability

a. Kernel
b. Class
c. Range
d. Bandwidth

8. A _____ is the result of applying a function to a set of data.

More formally, statistical theory defines a _____ as a function of a sample where the function itself is independent of the sample's distribution: the term is used both for the function and for the value of the function on a given sample.

A _____ is distinct from an unknown statistical parameter, which is not computable from a sample.

a. Statistic
b. Spatial dependence
c. Parameter space
d. Loss function

9. _____ is a mathematical science pertaining to the collection, analysis, interpretation or explanation, and presentation of data. It also provides tools for prediction and forecasting based on data. It is applicable to a wide variety of academic disciplines, from the natural and social sciences to the humanities, government and business.

a. Regression toward the mean
b. Probability distribution
c. Percentile rank
d. Statistics

10. The _____ or Dirac's delta is a mathematical construct introduced by the British theoretical physicist Paul Dirac. Informally, it is a function representing an infinitely sharp peak bounding unit area: a function that has the value zero everywhere except at x = 0 where its value is infinitely large in such a way that its total integral is 1. It is a continuous analogue of the discrete Kronecker delta.

a. Hyperfunction
b. Schwartz kernel theorem
c. Dirac delta
d. Weak derivative

11. A bar chart or _____ is a chart with rectangular bars with lengths proportional to the values that they represent. Bar charts are used for comparing two or more values. The bars can be horizontally or vertically oriented.

a. 1-center problem
b. Bar graph
c. 2-3 heap
d. 120-cell

12. In statistics, a _____ is a graphical display of tabulated frequencies, shown as bars. It shows what proportion of cases fall into each of several categories. A _____ differs from a bar chart in that it is the area of the bar that denotes the value, not the height as in bar charts, a crucial distinction when the categories are not of uniform width.
   a. Standardized moment
   b. Probability distribution
   c. First-hitting-time models
   d. Histogram

13. In geometry a _____ is traditionally a plane figure that is bounded by a closed path or circuit, composed of a finite sequence of straight line segments. These segments are called its edges or sides, and the points where two edges meet are the _____'s vertices or corners. The interior of the _____ is sometimes called its body.
   a. Parallelogon
   b. Regular polygon
   c. Polygon
   d. Polygonal curve

14. _____ are used in computer graphics to compose images that are three-dimensional in appearance. Usually triangular, _____ arise when an object's surface is modeled, vertices are selected, and the object is rendered in a wire frame model. This is quicker to display than a shaded model; thus the _____ are a stage in computer animation.
   a. Triskaidecagon
   b. Visibility polygon
   c. Polygons
   d. Heptadecagon

15. In mathematics, an _____, or central tendency of a data set refers to a measure of the 'middle' or 'expected' value of the data set. There are many different descriptive statistics that can be chosen as a measurement of the central tendency of the data items.

An _____ is a single value that is meant to typify a list of values.

a. A posteriori
b. A chemical equation
c. A Mathematical Theory of Communication
d. Average

16. In statistics, _____ has two related meanings:

- the arithmetic _____.
- the expected value of a random variable, which is also called the population _____.

It is sometimes stated that the '_____' _____s average. This is incorrect if '_____' is taken in the specific sense of 'arithmetic _____' as there are different types of averages: the _____, median, and mode. For instance, average house prices almost always use the median value for the average.

For a real-valued random variable X, the _____ is the expectation of X.

a. Probability
b. Statistical population
c. Proportional hazards model
d. Mean

17. In geometry, a _____ of a triangle is a line segment joining a vertex to the midpoint of the opposing side. Every triangle has exactly three _____s; one running from each vertex to the opposite side.

The three _____s are concurrent at a point known as the triangle's centroid, or center of mass of the triangle.

a. Median
b. Percentile rank
c. Statistical significance
d. Correlation

18. In mathematics, the _____ of a real number is its numerical value without regard to its sign. So, for example, 3 is the _____ of both 3 and −3.

The _____ of a number a is denoted by | a | .

Generalizations of the _____ for real numbers occur in a wide variety of mathematical settings.

Chapter 10. Statistics and Probability

a. Area hyperbolic functions
b. A Mathematical Theory of Communication
c. A chemical equation
d. Absolute value

19. In statistics, the _____ is the value that occurs the most frequently in a data set or a probability distribution. In some fields, notably education, sample data are often called scores, and the sample _____ is known as the modal score.

Like the statistical mean and the median, the _____ is a way of capturing important information about a random variable or a population in a single quantity.

a. Deltoid
b. Mode
c. Field
d. Function

20. In descriptive statistics, a _____ is any of the three values which divide the sorted data set into four equal parts, so that each part represents one fourth of the sampled population.

- first _____ = lower _____ = cuts off lowest 25% of data = 25th percentile
- second _____ = median = cuts data set in half = 50th percentile
- third _____ = upper _____ = cuts off highest 25% of data, or lowest 75% = 75th percentile

The difference between the upper and lower _____s is called the interquartile range.

There is no universal agreement on choosing the _____ values.

The formula for the position of the observation at a given percentile, y, with n data points sorted in ascending order is:

$$L_y = (n+1)\left(\frac{y}{100}\right)$$

Example 4.
a. Trimean
b. Quartile
c. Mean reciprocal rank
d. Seven-number summary

Chapter 10. Statistics and Probability

21. A _____ is is a graphical technique for presenting a data set drawn by hand or produced by a mechanical or electronic plotter. It is a graph depicting the relationship between two or more variables used, for instance, in visualising scientific data.

_____s play an important role in statistics and data analysis.

a. C-35
b. Lattice
c. Dini
d. Plot

22. In descriptive statistics, the _____ middle fifty and middle of the #s, is a measure of statistical dispersion, being equal to the difference between the third and first quartiles.

Unlike the range, the _____ is a robust statistic, having a breakdown point of 25%, and is thus often preferred to the total range.

The IQR is used to build box plots, simple graphical representations of a probability distribution.

a. A Mathematical Theory of Communication
b. Unitized risk
c. A chemical equation
d. Interquartile range

23. In probability and statistics, the _____ is a measure of the dispersion of a collection of numbers. It can apply to a probability distribution, a random variable, a population or a data set. The _____ is usually denoted with the letter σ.
a. Null hypothesis
b. Standard deviation
c. Failure rate
d. Statistical population

24. In mathematics and statistics, _____ is a measure of difference for interval and ratio variables between the observed value and the mean. The sign of _____, either positive or negative, indicates whether the observation is larger than or smaller than the mean. The magnitude of the value reports how different an observation is from the mean.
a. Deviation
b. Filter
c. Conchoid
d. Functional

25. In scientific inquiry, an _____ is a method of investigating particular types of research questions or solving particular types of problems. The _____ is a cornerstone in the empirical approach to acquiring deeper knowledge about the world and is used in both natural sciences as well as in social sciences. An _____ is defined, in science, as a method of investigating less known fields, solving practical problems and proving theoretical assumptions.
   a. A Mathematical Theory of Communication
   b. A chemical equation
   c. A posteriori
   d. Experiment

26. In game theory, an _____ is a set of moves or strategies taken by the players, or their payoffs resulting from the actions or strategies taken by all players. The two are complementary in that given knowledge of the set of strategies of all players, the final state of the game is known, as are any relevant payoffs. In a game where chance or a random event is involved, the _____ is not known from only the set of strategies, but is only realized when the random even are realized.
   a. Equaliser
   b. Algebraic
   c. Autonomous system
   d. Outcome

27. _____ is the likelihood or chance that something is the case or will happen. Theoretical _____ is used extensively in areas such as statistics, mathematics, science and philosophy to draw conclusions about the likelihood of potential events and the underlying mechanics of complex systems.

The word _____ does not have a consistent direct definition.

   a. Statistical significance
   b. Standardized moment
   c. Discrete random variable
   d. Probability

28. In statistics, a _____ is a subset of a population. Typically, the population is very large, making a census or a complete enumeration of all the values in the population impractical or impossible. The _____ represents a subset of manageable size.
   a. Dispersion
   b. Boussinesq approximation
   c. Duality
   d. Sample

Chapter 10. Statistics and Probability

29. In probability theory, the _____ or universal _____, often denoted S, Ω of an experiment or random trial is the set of all possible outcomes. For example, if the experiment is tossing a coin, the _____ is the set {head, tail}. For tossing a single six-sided die, the _____ is {1, 2, 3, 4, 5, 6}.
   a. Markov chain
   b. Martingale central limit theorem
   c. Marginal distribution
   d. Sample space

30. In probability theory, an _____ is a set of outcomes to which a probability is assigned. Typically, when the sample space is finite, any subset of the sample space is an _____. However, this approach does not work well in cases where the sample space is infinite, most notably when the outcome is a real number.
   a. Event
   b. Information set
   c. Audio compression
   d. Equaliser

31. Any mathematical statement that contains a variable is a _____.
   a. Classification of the finite simple groups
   b. Variable expression
   c. Complex Mexican hat wavelet
   d. Convex and concave

32. In mathematics and in the sciences, a _____ (plural: _____e, formulæ or _____s) is a concise way of expressing information symbolically (as in a mathematical or chemical _____), or a general relationship between quantities. One of many famous _____e is Albert Einstein's $E = mc^2$ (see special relativity

In mathematics, a _____ is a key to solve an equation with variables. For example, the problem of determining the volume of a sphere is one that requires a significant amount of integral calculus to solve.

   a. Formula
   b. 1-center problem
   c. 2-3 heap
   d. 120-cell

33. The word _____ denotes information gained by means of observation, experience as opposed to theoretical. A central concept in science and the scientific method is that all evidence must be _____ that is, dependent on evidence or consequences that are observable by the senses. It is usually differentiated from the philosophic usage of empiricism by the use of the adjective '_____' or the adverb 'empirically.' '_____' as an adjective or adverb is used in conjunction with both the natural and social sciences, and refers to the use of working hypotheses that are testable using observation or experiment.
   a. A chemical equation
   b. Empirical
   c. A posteriori
   d. A Mathematical Theory of Communication

34. _____ or experimental probability, is the ratio of the number favorable outcomes to the total number of trials , not in a sample space but in an actual sequence of experiments. In a more general sense, _____ estimates probabilities from experience and observation. The phrase a posteriori probability has also been used an alternative to _____ or relative frequency.
   a. A posteriori
   b. A Mathematical Theory of Communication
   c. A chemical equation
   d. Empirical Probability

35. In the physical sciences, _____ is a measurement of the gravitational force acting on an object. Near the surface of the Earth, the acceleration due to gravity is approximately constant; this means that an object's _____ is roughly proportional to its mass.

In commerce and in many other applications, _____ means the same as mass as that term is used in physics.

   a. 1-center problem
   b. 120-cell
   c. 2-3 heap
   d. Weight

36. In probability theory and statistics the _____ in favour of an event or a proposition are the quantity p /, where p is the probability of the event or proposition. The _____ against the same event are / p. For example, if you chose a random day of the week, then the _____ that you would choose a Sunday would be 1/6, not 1/7.
   a. Event
   b. Estimation of covariance matrices
   c. Anscombe transform
   d. Odds

37. A _____, from the French patron, is a type of theme of recurring events of or objects, sometimes referred to as elements of a set. These elements repeat in a predictable manner. It can be a template or model which can be used to generate things or parts of a thing, especially if the things that are created have enough in common for the underlying _____ to be inferred, in which case the things are said to exhibit the unique _____.
   a. 1-center problem
   b. 2-3 heap
   c. 120-cell
   d. Pattern

38. A _____ is the sum of the n natural numbers from 1 to n.

$$T_n = 1 + 2 + 3 + \cdots + (n-1) + n = \frac{n(n+1)}{2} = \frac{n^2+n}{2} \overset{\text{def}}{=} \binom{n+1}{2}$$

As shown in the rightmost term of this formula, every _____ is a binomial coefficient: the nth triangular is the number of distinct pairs to be selected from n + 1 objects. In this form it solves the 'handshake problem' of counting the number of handshakes if each person in a room full of n+1 total people shakes hands once with each other person.

   a. Heptagonal number
   b. Centered pentagonal number
   c. Star number
   d. Triangular number

39. In mathematics, a _____ is an algebraic structure consisting of a set together with an operation that combines any two of its elements to form a third element. To qualify as a _____, the set and operation must satisfy a few conditions called _____ axioms, namely associativity, identity and invertibility. While these are familiar from many mathematical structures, such as number systems--for example, the integers endowed with the addition operation form a _____--the formulation of the axioms is detached from the concrete nature of the _____ and its operation.
   a. Characteristic function
   b. Derivative algebra
   c. Group
   d. Coherence

40. _____ is a two-player mathematical game of strategy in which players take turns removing objects from distinct heaps. On each turn, a player must remove at least one object, and may remove any number of objects provided they all come from the same heap.

Variants of _____ have been played since ancient times.

a. Ghost Leg
b. 1-center problem
c. Subtract-a-square
d. Nim

ANSWER KEY

Chapter 1
1. a   2. b   3. d   4. c   5. c   6. c   7. a   8. d   9. a   10. c
11. d   12. a   13. d   14. b   15. b   16. d   17. d   18. c   19. d   20. d
21. d   22. a   23. d   24. c   25. c   26. d   27. d   28. d   29. c   30. d
31. d   32. d   33. c   34. b   35. d   36. d   37. a   38. a   39. a   40. d
41. b   42. c   43. d   44. b   45. b   46. d   47. b   48. a   49. b   50. d
51. b   52. d   53. b   54. b   55. a   56. a   57. d   58. d   59. d   60. d
61. d   62. d   63. c   64. d   65. d

Chapter 2
1. d   2. d   3. d   4. c   5. a   6. d   7. a   8. d   9. d   10. d
11. d   12. a   13. d   14. b   15. d   16. a   17. a   18. d   19. d   20. d
21. d   22. d   23. d   24. c   25. d   26. d

Chapter 3
1. a   2. c   3. d   4. c   5. d   6. c   7. d   8. b   9. d   10. b
11. d   12. d   13. d   14. d   15. d   16. d   17. a   18. d   19. d   20. b
21. a   22. a   23. d   24. d   25. a   26. b   27. d   28. d   29. c   30. a
31. b

Chapter 4
1. d   2. d   3. d   4. d   5. d   6. d   7. d   8. b   9. d   10. a
11. d   12. b   13. c   14. d   15. b   16. d   17. b   18. d   19. d   20. b
21. a   22. a   23. d   24. c   25. d   26. d   27. c   28. c   29. a   30. c

Chapter 5
1. a   2. d   3. d   4. b   5. b   6. d   7. d   8. d   9. a   10. d
11. a   12. d   13. d   14. b   15. b   16. d   17. b   18. d   19. d   20. d
21. c   22. d   23. b   24. d   25. d   26. d   27. d   28. c   29. b   30. c

Chapter 6
1. c   2. a   3. a   4. c   5. b   6. d   7. a   8. d   9. d   10. a
11. d   12. d   13. c   14. d   15. d   16. a   17. a   18. a   19. d   20. c
21. a   22. b   23. d   24. d   25. d   26. d   27. a   28. b   29. a   30. c
31. d   32. d   33. d

Chapter 7
1. d   2. d   3. a   4. a   5. a   6. d   7. a   8. d   9. c   10. a
11. a   12. c   13. b   14. d   15. b   16. b   17. d   18. d   19. a   20. d
21. d   22. d

Chapter 8
1. b   2. d   3. c   4. b   5. d   6. d   7. d   8. d   9. d   10. c
11. d   12. d   13. c   14. d   15. d   16. d

Chapter 9

1. b	2. d	3. c	4. d	5. d	6. d	7. d	8. d	9. b	10. a
11. d	12. a	13. d	14. d	15. c	16. b	17. c	18. a	19. b	20. c
21. c	22. d	23. a	24. a	25. b	26. d	27. b	28. d	29. d	30. d
31. b	32. d	33. d	34. d	35. c	36. d	37. a	38. d	39. b	40. a
41. a	42. d	43. d	44. d	45. d	46. c	47. d	48. d	49. d	50. b
51. a	52. c	53. d	54. b	55. c	56. c	57. d	58. d	59. d	60. b
61. d	62. b	63. d	64. b	65. a	66. d	67. a	68. b	69. a	70. d
71. a	72. b	73. b	74. a	75. b	76. d	77. d	78. d	79. b	80. b
81. a									

Chapter 10

1. d	2. b	3. c	4. b	5. d	6. a	7. c	8. a	9. d	10. c
11. b	12. d	13. c	14. c	15. d	16. d	17. a	18. d	19. b	20. b
21. d	22. d	23. b	24. a	25. d	26. d	27. d	28. d	29. d	30. a
31. b	32. a	33. b	34. d	35. d	36. d	37. d	38. d	39. c	40. d

www.ingramcontent.com/pod-product-compliance
Lightning Source LLC
Chambersburg PA
CBHW082048230426
43670CB00016B/2818